M-MAT

Multi-Modal

Attachment Therapy

M-MAT
Multi-Modal
Attachment Therapy

Healing Attachment Injuries in Children and Families

CATHERINE A. YOUNG

Granite Swan Press
Groveland, CA

For permission contact: permissions@graniteswanpress.com

ISBN 978-1-7335703-1-2
ISBN 978-1-7335703-0-5 (ebook)

Library of Congress Control Number 2019900523

Excerpt from article, "Bonding and Attachment in Maltreated Children," by Bruce Perry, MD, Ph.D. (childtrauma.org).
Reprinted by permission.

Published by Granite Swan Press
P.O. Box 122
Groveland CA 95321

Visit www.facebook.com/MultiModalAttachmentTherapy

Visit www.m-mat.org

Visit www.graniteswanpress.com

This book is dedicated to all of the creative and caring therapists who walk with children and families on their healing journeys, and the courageous children and families who allow us to walk with them. I have been privileged to know a few!

Contents

Acknowledgements

It takes the courage of people putting their ideas on paper throughout the years to allow therapies to develop and evolve. I wish to acknowledge all those who have done so, and so have, in their own way, contributed to this work. These include, among others, Carl Rogers with his discussions of unconditional positive regard, empathy, and authenticity, which still set the foundation for many therapies today; Mary Ainsworth and John Bowlby, who brought the concept of attachment to the fore; Cloe Madanes with her work with families impacted by abuse; and Daniel Hughes, Ph.D., Bruce Perry, MD, Ph.D., and Daniel Siegel, MD, whose more recent works bring contemporary ideas to the treatment of children and families.

I would further like to acknowledge the architects of Narrative Therapy, Theraplay®, and Cognitive Behavioral Therapy, whose contributions are evident in my work.

I've come to know these therapies and individuals through trainings and writings, and I am grateful to all. I've attempted to give credit, where due, throughout the book.

Finally, I would like to acknowledge Lisa, Jennifer and Martin for their unerring editorial acumen, and Whitney and Ben for their input and support.

Introduction

Children struggling with attachment injuries are often sad, angry, anxious, depressed, hurting and hurtful to others but, unfortunately, they are not very responsive to traditional child therapies. These children have been deeply injured in the first few years of their lives in their primary relationship; the relationship that is supposed to support, protect and nurture their young selves. They are struggling, and yet they reject the very things they need for healing: love, relationship and connection. This presents special challenges for both parents and therapists.

There is a strong need for a systematic, teachable, reproducible, effective and efficient therapy model to help these struggling children grow into healthy, happy adults. Multi-Modal Attachment Therapy (M-MAT) strives to be that model.

I do not pretend to bring entirely new concepts or thoughts to the field of child and attachment therapy, but rather to reorganize and integrate the information and words of others into a new, systematic and effective approach for working with the most troubled children. Multi-Modal Attachment Therapy (M-MAT) blends a variety of modalities, and adds new shadings and meanings, to create a whole that is much greater than the sum of its parts.

I have worked as a therapist with children with severe emotional/behavioral concerns, and their families, for well over twenty years. I have further supported other therapists in their work with children and families in my role as a clinical supervisor. One of my first clinical jobs after graduate school was in a public mental health day treatment program for children 7 to 12 years of age. Many of these children were one step away from being removed from their homes due to their behavioral/emotional difficulties. Up to that point, the training I had received and the reading I had done in child therapy had been in non-directive play therapy and behavior therapy. I soon found that these children needed something much more. They needed more structure, more relationship focus, and more direction to help them move out of destructive patterns and cycles.

I went in search of more effective therapies. I learned EFT (Emotional Freedom Technique) and EMDR (Eye Movement Desensitization and Reprocessing) which I often found helpful in reducing trauma symptoms in children. I was also excited to discover Narrative Therapy which provided a useful framework and interventions for helping children re-story their lives. When I discovered attachment therapies, I began to see hope for developing a consistently effective and efficient therapy to help these children and create the kind of pervasive, second order change I was looking for.

I studied, read books, and attended seminars and workshops in attachment therapy. The earliest targeted attachment therapies that I am aware of included the controversial holding therapy, and other practices, that led many to be concerned. Early attachment therapies seemed to go to an extreme in being directive and controlling.

Perhaps this was in response to the frustration and futility of utilizing non-directive therapies in addressing attachment injuries in children; or to these children's own frequent, highly controlling behaviors.

I was then exposed to therapists like Daniel Hughes, Ph.D., and Daniel Siegel, MD, who had much gentler approaches with positive results. I further attended a two-day workshop on Theraplay®, and was introduced to the concept of attachment-based play. Once I combined attachment-based play elements with an attachment focused, narrative, cognitive behavioral talk portion, I began to see more lasting, transformational changes in the children I worked with. I was further able to observe the same kinds of transformational changes in the clients of the therapists I was able to coach in this model.

I have taken elements of attachment-based play, other attachment-based therapies, cognitive behavioral therapy, narrative therapy, play therapy, solution focused therapy and, I am sure, other therapy modalities that I have absorbed over the years, and brought them together in a new, organized and systematic approach that I have found very effective in reaching these very challenging children.

Because it needs a name, I call this approach Multi-Modal Attachment Therapy (M-MAT). I call it Multi-Modal Attachment Therapy simply because it integrates a variety of therapeutic modalities in a systematic way to treat children with significant attachment injuries.

I have watched children transform from detached, angry, aggressive, emotionally disorganized, sometimes bizarre, sometimes withdrawn beings into loving, happy, emotionally connected children. These children have historically been so challenging to treat that I have had parents tell me that other professionals have told them not to expect too much of their child; not to expect too much love, too much growth, too much connection from these injured children.

I have had adoptive parents come to me as a last resort. Though very much committed to their child, they do not know if they can continue to have their child in their home. They are losing hope. They have tried everything, including therapy, sometimes for years, to no avail. For the child, the loss of a loving home, the thing they most need for healing, is a tragedy with lasting, devastating effects for both the child and society at large. It is this that has motivated me to write this book with the hopes of rekindling hope for these families, healing for these children, and efficacy for the therapists working to help them.

1

Orientation to this Book

Scope and Limitations of this Book

This book is intended to be a practical manual for therapists in implementing Multi-Modal Attachment Therapy (M-MAT) in their practice. It also may hold some use for parents and other professionals in understanding attachment and approaches to working with children with attachment injuries. It includes a brief overview of attachment theory and a discussion regarding children struggling with attachment injuries, with perhaps some useful insights. These are not exhaustive discussions of these topics, as that is out of the scope of this book, and there are many good resources that cover this information. Even if one has studied these areas extensively, however, it will be useful to read these sections as the perspectives expressed in this book specifically inform this therapy model.

The bulk of this book is devoted to understanding the principles and practice of Multi-Modal Attachment

Therapy (M-MAT). M-MAT is designed for children 5 to 12 years of age who have at least one adult in their life who is both committed to them and able to participate in the therapy. Children in other circumstances and of other ages, however, can be treated using the M-MAT model with adjustments, some of which will be described later in this book.

One group that poses special challenges, is most at-risk, and most likely to fall through the cracks, is the subset of children who do not have an adult who is committed to them and/or is capable of participating in therapy. This can include foster children in temporary placements, children whose parents are absent or deceased, or children whose parents or caregivers have addiction issues or mental health issues that interfere with their ability to care for their child and/or participate in therapy with their child. Sometimes it includes an adoptive parent who is no longer committed to their adopted child, or a long-term guardian who is unwilling to participate in the therapy, perhaps due to his/her own attachment injuries.

These children can be treated with Multi-Modal Attachment Therapy Individual (M-MAT Individual) which is discussed in chapter 10 of this book. The M-MAT model is the foundational model, and understanding the principles and procedures of this model is fundamental to understanding how to work individually with attachment injured children. The M-MAT Individual model is an adaptation of the M-MAT model.

Terms

Throughout this book, the terms "caregiver" and "parent" will be used interchangeably to mean the child's primary caregiver(s), whether that is a relative, foster or adoptive parent, biological parent, or guardian. For ease of writing and reading, the terms parent and caregiver can mean either one or two caregivers.

I will also use the term attachment injury, rather than attachment disorder. Children with attachment injuries have a range of attachment difficulties, from mild to severe, with a variety of presentations. I like the term attachment injury because it separates the child from the injury and injuries can heal. Like the physical metaphor, some injuries require intervention to heal or heal well. Further, I feel the term "Reactive Attachment Disorder" is narrowly defined in the *Diagnostic and Statistical Manual of Mental Disorders, Fifth Edition* (DSM-5) and has developed a lot of emotionally charged associations over the years. "Disinhibited Social Engagement Disorder" (new to the DSM-5 and previously "Reactive Attachment Disorder, disinhibited type" in DSM-IV) likewise only describes one presentation of the attachment injured child.

I occasionally use the term "attachment injured child" to indicate a child with moderate to severe untreated attachment injuries. This is for ease of communication, and not an attempt to label children. All children are more than their struggles, including children struggling with attachment injuries. Like any child, a child with attachment injuries may be bright, or musical, or creative, or have a good sense of humor, or display any other number of strengths that are a part of the whole person.

In the discussion of attachment-based play, the terms "activities" and "games" will be used interchangeably to refer to attachment-based play activities as described in Chapter 5 and Appendix A.

For brevity's sake, Multi-Modal Attachment Therapy will often be referred to as M-MAT.

For ease of reading, singular they, and its derivatives (their, them), will be used as needed for gender neutral pronouns, consistent with spoken language and evolving written language norms, and in lieu of the more awkward "he or she" and derivatives.

Hopes for this Book

My first hope for this book is that the many talented, committed and creative therapists in the world are able to implement the principles and practices outlined in this book to provide healing for children and families.

My second hope is that researchers will be able to conduct rigorous studies to validate this model. I can only speak to my experiences as a therapist and clinical supervisor as to the validity of this model, and, in this age of evidence-based practices, research has become critical for the use of effective practices in many settings. M-MAT's highly structured nature lends itself to study and replication and it, therefore, is a good candidate for research.

2

Attachment Theory Overview

Attachment theory postulates that the attachment, or connection, that a child forms with their primary caregiver during the first three years of life has a dramatic and profound effect on that child's development. Emotional, behavioral, moral, and relational aspects of the child's life are greatly impacted by their first relationships.

Attachment is defined by Bruce Perry, MD, Ph.D., as an enduring emotional relationship with a specific person that brings safety, comfort, soothing and pleasure; and the loss or threatened loss of the person brings intense distress. Further, the child finds comfort and safety in the context of this relationship. Note that the relationship is enduring and emotional, and that it is with a specific person. For the infant to develop an appropriate attachment, there needs to be at least one specific, consistent person in their life that provides safety, soothing, comfort and pleasure. The first, or primary, attachment is usually between infant and mother and sets the template for all future attachments.

Bruce Perry, MD, Ph.D., succinctly ties attachment to early brain development in this passage from "Bonding and Attachment in Maltreated Children" (www.childtrauma.org):

> *The capacity and desire to form emotional relationships is related to the organization and functioning of specific parts of the human brain. Just as the brain allows us to see, smell, taste, think, talk and move, it is the organ that allows us to love -- or not. The systems in the human brain that allow us to form and maintain emotional relationships develop during infancy and the first years of life. Experiences during this early vulnerable period of life are critical to shaping the capacity to form intimate and emotionally healthy relationships.*

Thus, we can view attachment injuries as the underdevelopment of portions of the brain. This is useful when we think of treatment, and how to exercise those parts of the brain in order to increase the capacity for positive attachment.

Attachment refers not only to infant parent relationships, but to relationships with close friends, family and partners as well. It is the first relationships, however, that set the stage for the child's subsequent relationships. The quality and nature of a person's later attachments, or their ability to attach at all, is strongly dependent on their first, primary attachment.

Attachment is not something the child does, or the parent does. Rather, it is the connection that is developed through the reciprocal interaction between parent and child. When the child cries, the parent responds. When the parent makes silly noises, the child smiles. Ideally the parent is attuned to their child's signals, providing stimulation, comfort, and affection. Through positive interactions with their caregiver, the child forms a sense of self-worth, a sense of efficacy in the world, and a template for all future relationships.

A child's healthy attachment to their caregiver is instrumental in helping the child to develop a positive sense of self, the ability to regulate emotion, a strong moral compass, resiliency in the face of challenges, prosocial behavior and empathy towards others. Resiliency research indicates that even just one healthy attachment/relationship in a child's life has a strong impact on the child's resilience and well-being over time.

When a child's attachment has been significantly disrupted in the first few years of life and has not been treated, the child may face issues of low self-esteem, difficulty regulating emotions, and lack of empathy towards others. They may display disruptive, anti-social or even bizarre behaviors. Though these children may be bright, they will often struggle to cope with the challenges of life, and their ability to establish healthy relationships will be severely impaired. Anxiety, anger and depression are common. Those trying to parent these children often feel like failures as nothing seems to work. Many adoptive and foster family placements fail due to unaddressed attachment injuries. Attachment injuries can equally be a concern for children in their biological homes when there has been early disrupted attachment.

Many things can disrupt a child's attachment, including both caregiver factors and child factors. Caregiver factors include:

- Multiple, sequential caregivers - A child can benefit from multiple caregivers if these are co-occurring and consistent over time, as in an extended family. If multiple caregivers are sequential, however, such as a child moving from foster home to foster home, great damage can be done as each caregiver attachment is broken, one after the other. By definition, foster and adopted children have suffered attachment injury having lost at least one primary attachment. The more they move around from home to home, the greater the potential for injury.

- Impairment in the caregiver's ability to respond appropriately to the child - This may include anything from depression, illness, substance abuse, mental illness, domestic violence, prolonged separation, or a parent with their own attachment injuries impairing their ability to respond to their child.

- Parental abuse and neglect - Severe neglect can be even more damaging than abuse to a child's attachment. The child who is not responded to at all can be more injured in their attachment than the child who is responded to harshly. Perhaps one of the most difficult parenting patterns for a child to cope with is one of severe neglect with unpredictable, sporadic abuse.

- Custody issues may contribute to attachment difficulties - For instance, attachment injury can occur when the child moves from a more stable parent's home to a less stable parent's home. The child experiences abandonment by the relatively healthy parent to whatever dangers exist in the home of the unstable parent, thus impairing their attachment to both.

Child factors include:

- Anything that may impair a child's ability to respond to their caregiver including the child's illness, chronic pain, disability, or extended separation from their caregiver.

Although different children will respond differently, generally speaking, the more severe and pervasive the disruption, the higher the potential for harm. Not all children experiencing the above will have significant attachment injuries. There are protective factors such as other significant relationships, child temperament, and subsequent care, to name a few, that play a role in health and injury as well.

In addition to individual costs of attachment injuries, there are also societal costs. Social service, health and law enforcement costs can be related to attachment injured individuals. If left untreated, attachment injury is passed from generation to generation along with cycles of abuse and neglect. For every child that is able to heal from attachment injury, there is benefit to the child, the family, and society at large.

For the purposes of M-MAT, children with attachment difficulties will be defined as children with attachment injuries. The term attachment injury is more inclusive than attachment disorder and suggests a continuum of severity from mild to severe; and, like all injuries, there is an implied potential for healing.

3

Children with Attachment Injuries

Understanding Attachment Injuries in Children

When presenting on attachment theory and therapy, I only half-jokingly state that we all have attachment issues. Certainly, many people have early relational challenges with their parents. This is what can make even adult relationships so difficult. Most people, however, are able to work out their early relational issues throughout their lives and subsequent relationships, sometimes with the help of therapy. When the attachment injury is too severe, however, the child rejects exactly what it is they need for healing. One way to conceptualize an attachment disorder is as an anxiety disorder. The child becomes so anxious and phobic of relationships (while at the same time desperately needing healthy relationship) that they push away, in every way possible, from those who might help.

The first three years of a child's life are crucial in the development of appropriate attachments. Severe disruptions during this period can be very damaging. It can be difficult for caregivers to understand why the child is having such difficulties when they are now in a loving, supportive home. The problem is that the child holds in their body and mind the experience that relationships are hurtful, painful, and life threatening and, additionally, that there is something wrong with them. From a neuroscience perspective, the parts of the brain involved in healthy attachment are likely underdeveloped, so the capacity for connection is impaired.

Take the example of a child that for the first six months of life lived in a situation where the parent suffered from addiction and mental health disabilities. This parent was passed out when their child was crying for food or comfort. When awake, the parent was highly irritable and screamed at the baby when they fussed too much. The child was malnourished and underweight. Maybe the parent had a partner that was abusive to them.

Perhaps at six months, the baby is removed from the home due to severe neglect. The child is preverbal, but what they have already learned is that they have no power to control their environment (lack of responsiveness to their cries), and while there is a biological imperative for the infant to be close to the caregiver for survival, the infant has found that the caregiver has threatened their survival and is unsafe. It is unsafe to try and get needs met, but also unsafe not to. The infant has learned that the big people in their life are to be feared and avoided. In the new home, the baby may be very quiet, avoidant, fussy, or alternately clingy and avoidant.

The new parents receiving this beautiful baby into their home may have no idea of the injury done to the child and the potential impact on the child's life, much less how to best support healing for the child. Fortunately, the child is young, their brain is still very young, and if the parents are knowledgeable and skilled, there is a chance for healing. If not, the child may be set up for lifelong difficulties.

Imagine, further, that this child stayed in their biological home until they were 3 years old. Maybe the parent was sometimes OK, but most of the time wasn't. The child now has a schema for parent and relationship that includes unpredictable, dangerous, hurtful and unhelpful. The child has learned that it is up to their 3-year-old self to get even the most basic needs met. The child cannot count on anyone, and tied to this is the belief, because young children are egocentric, that it is their fault. Something is fundamentally wrong with them for their parent to behave this way. The child is NOT OK, NOT lovable. There is no joy in this child's life. The brain develops to 90% of its adult size by age three. In this case, this amazing brain development has largely centered on survival and creating this cognitive schema in order to understand and cope in the world.

Children with attachment injuries tend to have the following beliefs:

• Adults, at best, have nothing to offer emotionally and, at worst, are deeply hurtful.
• Relationships are unsafe, scary and anxiety provoking.
• The child is unloveable/bad.
• There is no one the child can depend on.

As a result, the child feels deeply alone, ungrounded, empty and anxious, but does not know what they are missing.

Although the child may not be consciously aware of them, these core beliefs about themselves, relationships and caregivers are very rigid and do not change easily.

They generate behavior that is self-defeating, destructive, perpetuates the faulty beliefs, and pushes away the very support they so desperately need. This behavior can include:

- Easily dysregulated/difficulty calming - This can include long temper tantrums and rages that can be highly disruptive to family functioning. Parents may report that they feel they need to walk on eggshells around their child. Difficulty in regulating emotions may stem from the lack of parental soothing and co-regulation when younger. Young children learn to regulate their emotions with support from their parents or primary caregivers. When they have not had that early parental support, they may not have the skills or brain development necessary for self-regulation.
- Rejects adult efforts to help them regulate - This can be very frustrating to parents trying to help their child, particularly when their efforts seem to make things worse.
- Will not seek out caregivers for comfort, sharing or support - Sometimes this child may appear pseudo mature, with a high level of independence and little need for their caregiver.
- Poor eye contact or eye contact on their terms only - One of a young child's primary ways of communicating and receiving information from their caregivers is through eye contact. In a healthy parent/infant interaction, the child will receive reassurance and validation from their parent through eye contact. Young children will also assess the safety of a situation with an eye contact check-in with their parent. In an unhealthy situation, when all the child has received through eye contact is anger and hurt, or eye contact has been absent altogether, they will stop engaging in this way.

- Primitive/injurious self-soothing behaviors - This may include behaviors such as scratching themselves when in high distress or head banging. An older child may revert to thumb sucking, rocking or other behaviors generally associated with younger children.
- Controlling behaviors - The child may seem to have a need to be in charge or in control of every instance, often with frequent challenging of, or arguing with, adults. The child that has experienced parents who were either incapable of being in control, or when in control, were scary and unsafe, has learned that to feel safe, they need to feel in control.
- Fragile ego, poor winner/poor loser - This child does not do well with competition. The core belief that they are not OK makes losing intolerable and winning something to brag about in an attempt to keep at bay their bad feelings about themselves. They may also be hypersensitive to any kind of criticism or negative feedback from both peers and adults for the same reason.
- Poor impulse control - The child may have difficulty thinking before acting, leading to difficulties in school, home and with peers.
- Hypervigilance - The child is usually quite aware of what is happening around them, being extremely alert to any possible threat or danger. Their very survival may have depended on being able to read the cues in their environment and caregivers.
- Aggression - Kicking, hitting, scratching and biting are not unusual. The child may also exhibit aggression towards pets and animals. Aggression may be due to emotional dysregulation, poor impulse control, re-enactment of their own trauma, and/or expression of anger in unhealthy ways.

- Splitting of adults - The child may work at splitting the adults in their life as a matter of course. This may be going to different adults to get different answers, or trying to get one adult to side with them against another adult (most often the primary caregiver).

- Eating issues/food hoarding - This may be related to early food deprivation and/or be symbolic of the nurturing they so desperately need. It is not unusual for parents or caregivers to find food stuffed in nooks and crannies in the child's bedroom, or for children to sneak out at night to raid the refrigerator or cabinets.

- Can be superficially charming - This is a strategy that may have helped ensure the child's survival and allowed them to get at least some of their needs met. This can be particularly frustrating to parents when their child is charming with everyone else, but angry, irritable and dismissive with them.

- Indiscriminate/poor boundaries with unfamiliar adults - The child may go to anyone. They may jump in a stranger's lap. The child is seeking safety in an unsafe manner, and, for the unaware adult, this behavior may seem endearing, but the connection does not go very deep. In this child's world, one adult is easily exchanged for another adult. There is no discrimination, no particular connection to one adult. This behavior also sets the child up to be further victimized.

- Lack of empathy - The child's belief in a hostile world, and that at the core they are not OK, and their own deep neediness, makes it difficult for them to have empathy towards others.

- Nonsense lying and storytelling - Most children lie for a reason, either to get (i.e., a sweet) or avoid (i.e., punishment) something. The attachment injured child may lie for no apparent reason. Parents may report that the child will insist that the sky is yellow, or make up a story about something that happened at school that never actually happened with no apparent goal or reason.

Sometimes they will tell very elaborate stories that are clearly not true. Sometimes these stories will have an ego protective or bolstering function, such as stories in which they beat up bad guys, or they have accomplished unrealistic things, or have possessions they do not have.

- Bizarre behaviors - These can include anything well outside the range of normal. An example might be a child who offers their urine to peers as "lemonade".

- Peer problems - Attachment injured children will often have one of three ways of being with peers: they may be easily victimized and picked on due to their low self-esteem; they may be the bully or aggressor, again due to their low self-esteem (and it may seem a good alternative to being a victim, as no one wants to be a victim); or they may not seem to care about their peer interactions at all due to their disconnect with people in general. Sometimes a child alternates between being a bully and a victim in their peer interactions. Sometimes children with attachment injuries will look to peers to meet their primary attachment needs. This is a strategy that is bound to fail as their peers are unable to provide them the nurturing, stability, limit setting and maturity that they need. They may present as a leader or follower in these situations.

- Anxiety and depression - Attachment injured children can also be highly anxious and often suffer from depression.

Of course, not all attachment injured children will have all of these behaviors and each child is unique. Below are a few examples of how significant attachment injuries may manifest in children:

- 12-year-old is bright but is a bully and overeats. Child is big and hurts other children in sneaky ways, i.e., pushing

and tripping, when no one is looking. Has no positive peer relationships. Appears to lack empathy. Attempts to control people and situations.
- 5-year-old has hour long rages. Hits, kicks, throws things, screams. Scratches self, threatens to jump out of a window. Difficulty with both family and peer relations. Highly sensitive to perceived peer rejection.
- 11-year-old engages in nonsensical lying, baffling caregivers. Child has no peer connections, does not seem to want friends, and acts bizarrely with peers, i.e., offering dead bugs to eat as candy.
- 9-year-old attempts to push infant sibling out second story window. Avoids eye contact. Sneaks out of bedroom at night. Hoards food.
- 4-year-old is bright and makes everything a battle. Argues about everything. Refuses cooperation with even simple tasks. Rages for extended periods. Is a master at engaging parents in nonsensical arguments.
- 13-year-old runs from home often. "Hates" parent. Gets in trouble with peers. Is very promiscuous with unsafe sexual behaviors. Easily emotionally dysregulated wherein screams and yells and runs. Has tried various drugs. Is fully out of parental control. Sees any attempt of parent to help as an attempt to hurt.
- 8-year-old seems cute and charming outside the home, but regularly assaults parent in the home, hitting, kicking, and scratching, leaving bruises and marks.

The attachment injured child is likely to display their most challenging behaviors with their primary caregiver, usually the mother. All the rage, anger and hurt is directed at the symbol of the person who was supposed to love them and be there for them unconditionally. Sometimes they appear to function well with others or in other settings, so that people begin to question the mother or primary caregiver's competence. It is not at all unusual for the mother or primary caregiver to be blamed by others for the child's difficulties with the reasoning that the child, "Does not behave that way with me!"

Although the assessment of Reactive Attachment Disorder and attachment injuries is beyond the scope of the book, attachment injuries are often evident from the first meeting with parent and child. Some obvious signs that there are attachment issues afoot:

- The child comes into the room for the first time and never references the parent. The child never looks at or to the parent, and never asks anything of the parent. The child may play with toys in the room, but does not try in any way to engage the parent. This child may try to engage the therapist while ignoring the parent, or may ignore the adults in the room altogether.
- The child is excessively familiar with the therapist physically and/or verbally, i.e., the child meets the therapist for the first time and tries to give the therapist a hug, or jump on the therapist's lap, or says they love the therapist.
- The child displays excessively controlling behavior, trying to control the parent's behavior, the situation, the therapy and the therapist.

Worldview of Children with Attachment Injuries

To understand the child's behavior and why traditional therapies have so often failed children with attachment injuries, it is useful to go further into the worldview of the attachment injured child.

To borrow a concept from Narrative Therapy, the attachment injured child has organized their experiences into a story or narrative in which parents, at best, have nothing to offer and, at worst, are deeply hurtful. Even when now placed in a new environment with loving parents, the child sees only the facts and incidents that fit with the initial story, or will bend and interpret facts to fit within that framework. The child holds a rigid and dysfunctional template for relationships.

In addition, when there has been severe neglect or an inconsistent, chaotic early environment, the child has not learned that what they do actually matters or makes a difference. The child has no sense of efficacy. The child does not develop a good understanding of cause and effect. Research confirms that children who experience early trauma have a deficit in their cause and effect reasoning.

Furthermore, the child feels deeply alone. There is no one the child can depend on. This creates a great deal of anxiety. In order to ward off this anxiety, the child often tries to control the environment and, even more strongly, tries to control interactions with the primary caregiver. The high anxiety associated with relationship, and the rigidity of the child's relational template, cause the child to push away from the things they need most for healing, closeness and attachment, keeping the attachment injured child in a state of disconnect.

Attachment Injured Children and Behavior

While parents would like their children to behave because it is the right thing to do, many children, but especially attachment injured children, are not that advanced in their thinking or moral development. For children with attachment injuries, anger, anxiety, hurt, and low self-worth all contribute to lashing out. Poor impulse control and poor self-regulation are likely contributing factors as well. These children may also be re-enacting abuse experienced by themselves or observed in their early years.

In the worldview of a child with attachment injuries, they are not OK, and the people around them are not OK, therefore there is little motivation to behave. Also supporting problematic behavior may be a strong sense of power achieved by acting out either aggressively or passive aggressively. For children with attachment injuries, this is a defense against the extreme powerlessness and fear they experienced when very young. It is not unusual to find that the whole household is run around the child's extreme behaviors. When that happens, it only feeds the maladaptive behavior.

Attachment injured children also may have had no structure, limits, or boundaries in the earliest part of their lives, and so are like untamed beings with the expectation of doing what they want when they want, and thus can perceive any kind of parental boundaries or limits as the parent wanting to unfairly control them.

Attachment injured children do not readily take responsibility for their behavior. Of course, many children avoid responsibility for wrongdoing so as to avoid getting in trouble or due to feelings of guilt or shame. The attachment injured child, however, may take this to an extreme. This will include lying when the evidence of their wrongdoing is incontrovertible (while their hand is still in the proverbial cookie jar). They may stick to their lie no matter what, blaming others and throwing a tantrum when caught or questioned.

This is likely a defense against intolerable feelings of shame they may feel when caught and/or the fear of getting in trouble. It is possible that getting in trouble, when the child was very little, led to physical and/or verbal abuse, which may have been life threatening, or perceived by the child as life threatening.

The Failure of Traditional Therapies with Attachment Injured Children

The dysfunctional relational template, and impaired cause and effect reasoning of attachment injured children, are largely responsible for why they do not respond well to traditional behavioral interventions. In fact, behavioral interventions can make the child worse because the child will interpret consequences as another injustice done to them, consistent with the initial narrative of their lives, and positive reinforcers as an attempt to control them. Positive reinforcers, often treats, desired objects or privileges, sometimes do not work at all, because the child's perceived need for control far outweighs the reward. The child may view a behavior plan as an attempt to control them, and giving up control, in their body/mind schema, is dangerous. Other times the child may comply temporarily in order to obtain the reinforcer, but then fall right back into previous behavior, because the forces driving the behavior are still present.

For behavioral interventions to work, the child must believe, deep down, that the caregiver has their best interest at heart and must be able to connect their behavior to consequences and rewards in a cause and effect manner. If not, behavioral interventions become a game and a power struggle between child and caregiver. If the child cannot rebel directly, the child will become sneaky and get back at the caregiver in sneaky or passive aggressive ways.

For example, when a parent tries to give the child a time out in their room for behavior, the child may have little sense that they created the time out by their behavior.

Rather, they believe the parent is being 'mean' and does not like them, which generates anger, hurt, and the continued belief that they are bad, further generating extreme and difficult behavior. If the parent is using a reward system, the child may feel that the parent is trying to control them. They may go along until they get the desired reward and then act out, or, if they do not earn the reward, they again may feel the parent is being mean to them. Alternately, the reward may have little meaning for them at all. Their interpretations, of course, are consistent with the narrative through which they organize all of their experiences and information. Events inconsistent with the original narrative are either not noticed or misinterpreted. Thus, in spite of the parents' best efforts, the child gets worse over time rather than better.

A teenage youth may state, with genuine anger and hurt, that, when they were little, their parents removed all their toys from their room, only to share a moment later in the conversation that they routinely broke and threw their toys. Or, with the same deep hurt, relay that their parents took away all their privileges at a time when they were completely out of control, running the streets, doing drugs, lying, and disobeying all household rules. The hurt that they feel comes from their earliest sense of abandonment, fear and anger, the only lens through which they are able to view their later experiences. Therefore consequences, both natural and otherwise, feel like just another hurt that their parents or the world is inflicting upon them, strengthening an already negative worldview.

Another traditional child therapy is non-directive play therapy a la Virginia Axline. In non-directive play therapy, the child is largely left to their own devices with minimal structure and direction from the therapist. The therapist provides reflective and mirroring responses. This can be an effective therapy for many children and many situations.

For the attachment injured child, however, this too closely mirrors their earliest experiences of neglect. The child is still alone. The child is still without limits and structure and an adult to help make sense of their world. The mirroring and reflective responses that the therapist provides are not harmful, but are not enough to break through the initial narrative.

Sometimes, in non-directive play, the attachment injured child will move away from open ended imaginative play because it is too anxiety provoking. Sometimes the child will repeat a theme over and over again in a way that appears stuck. Other times, the child will be very controlling of the therapist in the play session, telling them what to do in every instance. And sometimes the child will enact in play a high level of violence that is repetitive, feels counterproductive, and never seems to get resolved.

I have had many parents bring their children to me after months or even years of therapy that has not succeeded in bringing about any significant positive change. The child is injured in the area of relationship; it is through relationship that the child needs to be healed. Hands-off, non-directive play therapy is insufficient in these circumstances. If healing occurs in this context, it is most likely due to the therapeutic relationship, but this is a long, long road. It is possible that a mildly attachment injured child with a non-directive play therapist could make some improvement over many years with the therapist, but then it likely would be primarily the safe, stable, long term relationship that is providing the healing. Far more often, this therapy fails to address the child's needs altogether.

Cognitive Behavioral Therapy (CBT) and skills based therapies (i.e., self-soothing skills, communication skills) are useful when integrated into a larger attachment-based therapy, as they are in M-MAT, but, by themselves, fall short with the attachment injured child. This is because they only address the issue from a cognitive, verbal perspective. Much of attachment injury is pre-verbal and body oriented. We know young children need touch, eye contact, and play, all nonverbal avenues of growth, for appropriate development and attachment.

For skill building based therapies, attachment injured children often will not cooperate. If they do cooperate in the session and learn some skills, they often will not apply them in real life situations. They hold the beliefs that their parent is trying to hurt them and that they are bad, and so they have no motivation to get their anger or behavior under control. Their anger and acting out may be the only sense of power and control they have in their lives and they are unwilling to give that up. They need to both change their underlying beliefs, and begin to experience a positive attachment before the skill building can be effective.

Yet another approach to treatment of these treatment resistant children is medication. It is not unusual for attachment injured children to be on any of a number of medications to help them to calm, to focus, and to reduce depression and anxiety and other symptoms. For some children medication seems to be helpful in conjunction with therapy, and a psychiatric referral is often in order. For no attachment injured child, however, is medication alone the answer. A relational injury requires a relational intervention. Of course, children's symptoms are often complex, and a thorough evaluation by a child psychiatrist can be very useful.

In summary, children with attachment injuries have traditionally been extremely difficult to treat due to their rigid core beliefs or worldview. Many traditional child therapies have their place and can be integrated into effective therapy, but only when attachment is put center stage in the therapy process as it is in Multi-Modal Attachment Therapy (M-MAT).

Attachment Injuries and Mental Health Diagnoses

The young child with significantly disrupted attachment will often respond in one of two ways with others, either with inhibited attachment or disinhibited attachment. In the *Diagnostic and Statistical Manual of Mental Disorders, Fifth Edition* (DSM-5), these are accounted for in Reactive Attachment Disorder and Disinhibited Social Engagement Disorder respectively.

Inhibited attachment: These children will act as if adults do not exist in their world. They have come to believe that adults have nothing to offer them. They do not come to adults for solace or safety or assistance. They do not look to adults for positive interactions of any kind. They have no positive expectations of adults. In their world, they have come to rely only on themselves.

Disinhibited attachment: These children will go to anyone at any time. They do not differentiate between the familiar and the stranger. They do not develop specific attachments to anyone. People are interchangeable. Although they can be charming, their relationships are superficial. They have learned to look everywhere and anywhere to try to get their physical and emotional needs met. They will often jump into the lap of a stranger or take the hand of someone they have never met while at the same time being emotionally avoidant of their caregiver. They are vulnerable to being victimized due to their neediness and lack of discrimination and are easily led into trouble by others.

The DSM-5 descriptions of these diagnoses are rather narrow and do not capture the wide range of behaviors seen in children with severely injured attachment (such as nonsense lying or controlling behaviors). Furthermore, the DSM-5 diagnoses focus on children up to 5 years of age and caution is suggested in making these diagnoses after age 5. Therefore, latency age children are not well accounted for in these diagnoses.

For these reasons, the broader terms "attachment injury" and "attachment injured child" are used throughout this book to refer to attachment disorders and children with significant attachment injuries.

Whether the child exhibits inhibited or disinhibited attachment patterns, their ability to form strong, positive, reciprocal relationships is severely impaired. Those trying to engage in relationship with them will often feel manipulated, because these children have not learned what it is to truly relate to another human being. Sadly, while these children may feel empty inside, they do not really know what they are missing.

There are a number of other mental health diagnoses commonly given to children with attachment injuries. Attachment injured children often meet the DSM-5 criteria for Disruptive Mood Dysregulation Disorder which is categorized as a depressive disorder. Eating, mood and anxiety disorders are also common as are Oppositional Defiant Disorder and Conduct Disorder. Posttraumatic Stress Disorder (PTSD) may be present, either diagnosed or undiagnosed. Attention Deficit Hyperactivity Disorder (ADHD) is sometimes attributed to these children.

There was a period when many attachment injured children were being diagnosed with the somewhat controversial Pediatric Bipolar Disorder. Subsequent research indicates that these children more likely suffered from a depressive disorder, which is now better captured in Disruptive Mood Dysregulation Disorder.

As children with attachment injuries get older, some may be identified with "borderline" or "narcissistic" or "antisocial" traits, and untreated attachment injuries may develop into personality disorders.

4

Multi-Modal Attachment Therapy (M-MAT) Overview

Multi-Modal Attachment Therapy (M-MAT) is a structured attachment therapy with the primary focus on healing attachment injuries through adult/child interactions, integrating both play and talk therapies.

Target Population

M-MAT as described in this book is designed for children 5 to 12 years of age who are struggling with attachment injuries, along with at least one adult caregiver committed to the child. This model can also be used with teens, with modification, and has been used successfully with a youth as old as 16 years. Work with teens will be discussed further in Chapter 9: Putting It All Together.

The parent involved in the therapy needs to be the primary caregiver for the child. This might be an adoptive parent, long term foster parent, relative caregiver (grandparent, aunt, uncle) or biological parent. Attachment and resiliency research tells us that even one strong positive attachment is protective. Once the child has developed a strong primary attachment, they will be in a better position to make positive connections with others. If there are two parents involved with the child, the work can be done with both of the parents, but it may be best to start with the primary caregiver and introduce the other parent further along in the therapy.

Unfortunately, not all children have a committed adult able to do this work. Fortunately, there is a variation of this model, M-MAT Individual, modified specifically for individual therapy with attachment injured children. See Chapter 10: M-MAT Individual.

Concepts

The following are key concepts of Multi-Modal Attachment Therapy (M-MAT). How these are implemented in the therapy will become clearer in the following chapters.

1. The primary focus of healing in M-MAT is relational. The goal of the therapy is to heal the attachment/ relational injuries so the child can then access all the resources that healthy attachment allows within him or herself, and with others, in order to reach their full potential as a human being.

2. M-MAT is a two-pronged approach with both a play and a talk component. The play component utilizes largely non-verbal forms of communication, connection and nurturing, such as mirroring, rhythm, touch and eye contact.

    The talk component engages the power of language and the child's thoughts by addressing cognitive distortions, responsibility, and self-concept through re-storying, skill building and psychoeducation, creating a new narrative in which the child can organize and make sense of his/her experiences in a healthy, adaptive way.

The two components together reinforce each other, allow for deeper integration and healing, and are far more powerful than either alone. Together they access many parts of the brain and harness the incredible healing power inherent in both left and right brain modalities. If we presume that the child with attachment injuries has parts of the brain that are underdeveloped, the parts associated with attachment and relationship, then the goal is to stimulate and develop these parts of the child's brain through experiences of play and talk. Both the play and talk components of M-MAT will be described in detail in further chapters.

3. M-MAT is a highly structured therapy. The sessions are structured with a very definite beginning, middle and end. This provides a sense of safety and predictability for the child, and is therapeutic, in and of itself, as it provides ritual and corrects the unpredictability and lack of structure in the child's early years.

4. M-MAT's focus is on the relationship between the child and caregiver. The therapist takes every opportunity in session to refocus the child in relation to the parent or caregiver. So, for instance, if a child asks the therapist a question that can be easily answered by the parent, the therapist will redirect the child to the parent. If the child is coming to the therapist for affection or nurturing, the therapist will redirect to the parent. If the therapist is working with a caregiver who is the child's mother or father, biological or adoptive, the therapist will address the parent in the parent/child session by "Mom" or "Dad" (or equivalent) to reinforce

the parent's role in the child's life. The focus is on the parent/child relationship. The therapy helps not only the child feel connected to the parent, but helps the parent connect to the child as well. The healing is in the relationship for all parties involved.

5. M-MAT is a regressive therapy. That is to say, in the therapy session, the child is allowed to regress to a younger age. Games are played that would often be associated with a younger child. The child's relational injuries occurred at a young age and the purpose of the therapy is to go back to address those early injuries. Children with significant attachment issues are already emotionally young, although they may appear pseudo-mature. It is important, however, to modify the activities and therapy based on the child's developmental age, needs and abilities.

    Some people may worry that the child will come out of the session in a permanently regressed state. Simply put, that does not happen. Occasionally the child may temporarily seek out younger activities, forms of nurturing, or display younger behavior. The caregiver is encouraged, within reason, to fulfill the needs the child is expressing. More commonly, the child will allow themselves to regress in the session, but outside the session, will actually begin to display a higher level of maturity than previously. As the course of therapy progresses, the child will catch up to their chronological age, maturing in their ability to engage in the talk portion of the therapy in-session and to handle life stressors outside of session.

6. M-MAT takes a hierarchical approach. In the session, the adults are in charge. These children need SOMEONE to be in charge. They have been left to their own devices way too long, and have developed pathology due to it. They are often extremely

controlling in an effort to create predictability and safety for themselves. It is up to the adults to create that predictability and safety. The child needs to learn that the adults can be in charge and it can be safe, and even FUN! Often, if the therapist comes in unprepared to the session or unsure what to do, the child will sense the uncertainty and try to take charge. A sign of progress in the therapy is the child's willingness to let go of control.

7. Along the same lines, M-MAT is a directive therapy. The parent and child have likely been struggling for a long time, and it is not doing them a service to have them try to figure it out themselves. If they knew how to make things better, they would have done so already. The child is generally emotionally bankrupt, and in fear relationally, without the resources (knowledge or skills) to do anything different. The parents are often frustrated and exhausted, and their usual parenting skills have not worked. Parents are often quite relieved to have someone help them understand what is happening and to give them skills to address it. That being said, it is always important to be sensitive to the parent's beliefs and to work with them collaboratively to achieve the best results. This is further explored in Chapter 8: Working with Parents.

8. Attachment-based play is a fundamental component of M-MAT. Attachment-based play (discussed in Chapter 5: M-MAT Play) provides the foundation for all of the other work in the therapy. It is a key in healing attachment injuries, and prepares and allows the child to do the other therapy work.

9. M-MAT endeavors to create a new story or narrative for the child that is adaptive and health promoting. This concept is borrowed from Narrative Therapy. The dominant or maladaptive story that organizes the

child's perceptions and filters their experiences usually includes such concepts as: I'm not loved or lovable; there is something wrong with me and/or the adults around me; I am all alone; bad things have happened because I'm bad; to get close is to get hurt, etc. M-MAT creates an alternative story in which the child recognizes that they are loved and lovable, and where relationships become a source of comfort and joy rather than fear and pain. In M-MAT, this is accomplished through both cognitive and experiential processes, including a re-telling of the child's life story (the attachment narrative), addressing key issues and misperceptions; noticing and focusing on evidence, current and past, that supports the new story; and creating new, alternate experiences in the therapy itself, while promoting such outside the therapy as well.

10. M-MAT is always respectful of child and parent. Although the adults are in charge, and this is a directive therapy, the child is always shown kindness and respect. The child is never forced or coerced into participating, or into anything else. The child is never shamed or made to feel bad for their struggles, although these struggles are addressed. The main tools for engagement and buy-in for the child are playful engagement, fun, deep empathy, reflection, and truth.

11. M-MAT requires time and consistency to be effective. While M-MAT is an efficient therapy in addressing attachment injuries relative to other therapies, it is not a brief therapy. Therapists should ask caregivers to give them 10 weeks to work with them and their child before judging if the therapy is working. By 10 weeks there should be evidence of change. There will likely, however, still be a lot of work to be done.

Additionally, consistency is crucial. The damage has been done, and at times self-perpetuated, over years.

Repetition of the positive interactions, the structure, the re-storying, and the skill building is necessary to sustain change. The therapy structure in the family session has to be absolutely consistent. It will not work to use the M-MAT structure one session and not the next. When therapists utilized the structure and the attachment narrative with attachment injured children for one or two sessions, then returned to a less structured format, the report was some positive change at the end of, or immediately following, the M-MAT sessions, but then quick regression. Remember that the attachment injured child's brain has been utilizing maladaptive neural pathways for a long time. The goal is to change or re-route those neural pathways. This requires repetition.

To sum up the concepts discussed:

1. The goal of M-MAT is to heal relational/attachment injuries to free the way for the child to develop to their full potential.
2. M-MAT is a two-pronged therapy, using both play and talk; healing through left and right brain functions.
3. M-MAT is highly structured allowing for safety, consistency and predictability.
4. M-MAT focuses on the parent/caregiver-child relationship and healing that relationship.
5. M-MAT is a regressive therapy, going back to address early relational wounding.
6. M-MAT is a hierarchical approach, promoting safety and reducing anxiety through re-establishing appropriate adult/child hierarchy.
7. M-MAT is a directive therapy.
8. Attachment-based play provides the foundation for healing in M-MAT.

9. M-MAT creates a new story or narrative for the child that is adaptive and healing.
10. M-MAT is always respectful of the child and caregiver.
11. M-MAT requires time and consistency to be effective.

Therapeutic Stance

Throughout the therapy the therapist wants to convey to the parent and child acceptance, curiosity and empathy. These are three of the four components described by Daniel Hughes, Ph.D., in his books on attachment therapy and Dyadic Developmental Psychotherapy as the central therapeutic stance in supporting healing for children and families. The fourth is playfulness, which is encompassed in the concepts of fun and play that are fully embraced in the attachment play portion of M-MAT and discussed in Chapter 5: M-MAT Play.

Acceptance and empathy have long been recognized by most as fundamental to the therapeutic relationship. Humanist psychologist Carl Rogers identified unconditional positive regard and empathy as two of the three necessary elements of the therapeutic relationship to promote healing, the third being congruence or authenticity. With acceptance or unconditional positive regard, the child and parent are accepted for who they are and where they are in their growth and development. Voice tone is often as important, if not more important, than the words used in conveying a sense of acceptance. Acceptance or unconditional positive regard forms the basis for the therapeutic relationship in M-MAT with both parent and child.

Throughout M-MAT, the therapist uses empathy and deep empathy for the child and parent. The therapist wants to convey to parent and child an understanding of how they are feeling, and where they are coming from. Empathy and deep empathy have been defined in many ways. For the purposes of M-MAT, empathy is defined as understanding how one would feel in someone else's situation. Deep empathy is defined as understanding how the other person feels in that situation. This definition of deep empathy is consistent with Carl Roger's definition of deep empathy as "...entering the private perceptual world of the other and becoming thoroughly at home in it."

For instance, if the therapist is a parent, and can relate to some of the parent's struggles, the therapist can easily empathize with the parent. If the therapist has had some experiences similar to the child, they can empathize with the child in their struggles. Often, however, the therapist's perspective is quite different from the child or parent's.

As an example, a parent may say about their child, "He always tries to disrupt everything. He wants to make us miserable!" The therapist, however, may perceive that the child is largely having difficulty self-regulating in unstructured settings. It might be tempting for the therapist to immediately correct the parent with the therapist's perception. It is more helpful, however, for the therapist to truly put him or herself in the parent's place and acknowledge where the parent is with a deep empathy statement such as, "It must be really hard to believe that your child is trying to make you miserable, trying to disrupt everything for you. I can see why you feel that way." The therapist can then give the parent a chance to respond and explore this. When the therapist makes a deep empathy statement, the therapist is not necessarily saying that they believe the parent's perception is the truth, but the therapist is acknowledging the parent's experience and saying that they understand it. The parent is then more likely to be open to the exploration of other perspectives or possibilities.

An example with the child might be when the child says of their parents, "They hate me!" The therapist may be aware that the parents care deeply for their child, but it is not useful to simply say, "No they don't, they love you very much!" Rather the therapist wants to view this as a distorted cognition that the child is carrying that is causing them a lot of distress. A deep empathy response would be, "Wow, that must be so hard to believe your parents, who should love and care for you, actually hate you. That would be very difficult to feel." Again, the therapist is not saying that it is true, simply that the therapist understands their perspective and how hard that must be.

Deep Empathy is discussed further in Chapter 7: M-MAT Talk, in the section on addressing behavior, and in Chapter 8: Working with Parents.

The talk portion of M-MAT can include a lot of questions by the therapist. An attitude of curiosity about the child and parent and their situation and responses demonstrates an interest in the child and parent and their experiences, while minimizing defensiveness on the clients' part.

Curiosity is non-judgmental. Using words like, "I'm wondering about..." and, "I'm curious about..." portray a sense of curiosity that minimizes defensiveness. Voice tone is very important and can convey a strong sense of curiosity. For instance, asking questions like, "So...are you saying that you have always loved Johnny?" with the right inflection of curiosity (higher pitch at the end of the question) can come across as a wondering on the therapist's part, rather than an inquisition or doubting the client.

So, with fun, acceptance, curiosity, and empathy the therapist joins with the family and child on a journey towards healing!

Structure

This section provides an overview of the session structure. Detailed interventions will be discussed in following chapters.

M-MAT consists of two types of sessions: Parent sessions and Parent/Child sessions. For the purpose of consistency, it is important that the parent/child sessions occur at least weekly. Initially, it is helpful for the separate parent sessions to occur weekly as well. Later in the therapy the parent sessions may be reduced in frequency, depending on parent need, as determined collaboratively with the parent. It may work well to have the parent session first, then, immediately following, have the child join the session for the parent/child component.

Parent Sessions

The parent sessions are an important part of the therapy. This is an opportunity to address parenting issues through the lens of attachment theory. Parents receive support, education and an opportunity to discuss concerns. Initially, parent sessions are weekly. It is a time when parents can review challenges that have come up during the week, can get the support they need, and can work on the parenting of their child.

Parents of attachment injured children often feel like failures, so psychoeducation and support for the parents can be critical to the child's success. This component includes the therapist and at least one caregiver. It is even better to have both caregivers when there are two caregivers involved. If there are other individuals, such as other family members or childcare providers, who provide care for the child, it can be useful on occasion to include them in a session as well to provide psychoeducation and develop consistent strategies across settings for working with the child.

Parent/Child Sessions

Parent/Child sessions are the heart of attachment therapy. Through attachment play and therapy, the reparative, healing work for the child is begun. These sessions include the therapist, child and one or two caregivers.

The parent/child sessions are highly structured. There is a distinct beginning, middle and end. The beginning and the end portions create the frame, which frames the middle talk section. Once the therapist has completed the assessment, if the therapist is not implementing the frame in every parent/child session, then they are not doing M-MAT. The parent/child session structure looks like this:

Beginning: Attachment-Based Play: The Frame Part 1
Middle: Attachment Talk (Re-Storying, Skill Building, Psychoeducation, Addressing Behavior)
End: Feeding and Attachment Questions:
    The Frame Part 2

Each of these parts has an entire chapter devoted to it, to describe the rationale, process and implementation in detail.

The following is an example of a typical parent/child therapy session:

Parent(s) and child come in and sit on the couch together. The therapist and family start out with attachment-based games. These games are designed to engage the child, provide nurturing and structure, encourage self-regulation, build trust and a sense of safety, and, most importantly, begin healing the attachment injury. Games always include at least one of four attachment elements: touch, eye contact, mirroring and/or rhythm. They may include:

- Follow the leader games (the adults in the room always start as the leaders, but the child always gets a turn to lead as well). These games allow the child to learn to follow an adult's lead in an enjoyable and positive way, and gives the child the chance to be followed or mirrored by caring adults.
- Touch games that are positive, non-intrusive and non-threatening such as clapping games, passing a 'touch' around the circle, thumb wrestling, or practicing a 'gentle touch' between parent and child. Positive touch is instrumental in healing for attachment injured children.
- Singing games that are adaptations of familiar songs (i.e., "Row Row Row Your Boat", "Twinkle Twinkle Little Star" or "Rock a Bye Baby") that express caring and nurturing for the child.
- Eye contact games (i.e., peek-a-boo for young children, seeing how long parent and child can look at each other without breaking eye contact for older children).

Children are at times gently assisted in participating, or encouraged to participate, but are never forced to engage. Being playful often draws them in, and, on occasions when they choose not to engage, parent and therapist continue the play until the child is ready to re-engage. In some cases the child will go through a phase of resistance to the therapy as they are resisting giving up control, or feeling more vulnerable than they like, but this is usually short lived. M-MAT attachment-based play is further defined and discussed in Chapter 5: M-MAT Play. A list of attachment-based play activities can be found in Appendix A.

After the play, the therapist facilitates talk about whatever is appropriate. This may include addressing/ understanding past history (attachment narrative) and re-storying, skill building, psychoeducation, and/or addressing current behavior. Details on attachment talk can be found in Chapter 7: M-MAT Talk.

The therapy session is concluded with the parent feeding their child a snack, and parent and child answering positive, attachment-based questions. The therapist provides small crackers or some kind of treat (that the child likes and the parent agrees to), which the parent feeds to the child as child and parent answer questions such as "What is one time that you had fun with your child this week?" Questions are always positive and success oriented. Thus the session is ended on a positive note. If appropriate, the child also has the opportunity to feed the parent, thus supporting reciprocal interaction. This feeding activity is described in more detail in Chapter 6: M-MAT Feeding and Questions.

These parent/child sessions usually occur once a week for approximately 50 minutes. The length of parent/child sessions, however, should be guided by the child's tolerance for the therapeutic interaction, and the material to be covered. Young children may do better with shorter, more frequent sessions.

Course of Therapy

Beginning Phase

The goals of the beginning phase of therapy are to assess, to get the parents on board, and to have the child at least minimally cooperating.

The child usually comes to therapy due to the parents' concerns. It is often best to conduct the first assessment session with the parents alone, so they can speak freely in expressing their concerns, and the therapist can obtain a good history. It is also important to meet with the parents alone, without their child, in order to form a partnership with them in helping their child.

The therapist can then see the child with the parents, and possibly the child by him or herself. The therapist should conduct a thorough child and family assessment in order to fully understand the child and family needs. There are many good child assessments available and it is beyond the scope of this book to go into detail regarding assessment. The therapist will want to make sure they observe parent/child interactions for attachment behaviors, or lack thereof.

Once the therapist has completed a thorough assessment, if the therapist determines that M-MAT is appropriate, they then meet with the parents alone to discuss the results of the assessment, determine the level of parenting support needed, explain attachment and M-MAT and get buy-in from the parents. The therapist should also ask the parents to allow the therapist to handle behaviors in the parent/child sessions, so as to avoid allowing children to power struggle with their parents or take control of the sessions. Let parents know that the initial work in therapy is on relationship building in session between them and their child. Parents are often relieved to be taken out of the disciplinarian role for this short period.

Additional parent-only sessions are designed around parent need. Therapist and parent can work on structure in the home, further psychoeducation, attachment-based parenting, and parent support, as needed.

The beginning phase of the parent/child sessions should be very short, only one to three weeks. The initial Parent/ Child sessions focus on engagement and activities oriented toward the child experiencing success and fun. Generally, sessions in the early phase of treatment involve more attachment-based play and less talk than in later phases of treatment. The first session may be limited to attachment-based play and the feeding and questions portions. The initial goal may be simply to engage the child positively. The story of love intervention as described in the talk therapy section is the first talk intervention and can be done in the initial phase of therapy. The therapist, in collaboration with the parent, is always in charge of the session, determining what activities to initiate.

Later in treatment, when the child is demonstrating more integration of the self, the therapy will usually involve more cognitive work. Always, though, the same structure of the therapy is kept throughout, starting with M-MAT play and ending with M-MAT feeding and questions.

Sometimes therapists make the mistake of extending the beginning phase too long. When issues are not being actively addressed, the child and parent may get bored, the child will more likely act out in the session, and rapport can be lost. Parents have said that they addressed more in the first few weeks of M-MAT than they did in many months of other therapies. Once the child and parent are familiar with the structure, it is time to move on to the middle phase.

Middle Phase

The middle phase of the therapy is where the major work is done. Attachment play is continued throughout to address the non-verbal needs of the child. Additionally, issues are addressed directly through talk therapy. Historical issues are addressed first using the story of love, and then the attachment narrative as described in Chapter 7: M-MAT Talk. Once the child's story has been told, with deep empathy and corrective cognitions, skill building and current behavior can more easily be addressed.

The therapist can expect some resistance from the child to surface in the middle phase of therapy. It is good to prepare parents ahead of time for this possibility. If the structure is consistent and maintained throughout, resistance tends to be brief.

In the parent only sessions, the therapist should be working with the parents on developing a support system; establishing positive touch and one-on-one time outside of the session; and working on parenting skills.

By week 10 of the parent/child therapy, parents should be reporting some positive changes in attachment and behavior for their child. This is not a brief therapy, yet there should be enough change or indicators at this point to give the parent enough hope and motivation to continue the therapy. If not, the situation needs to be reassessed. The middle phase of therapy can last anywhere from six months to several years, depending entirely on the progress and needs of the child and family

Last Phase

The therapist will know that they are reaching the last phase of the therapy when the child is no longer trying to control the session, behaviors are under control, parents feel competent in parenting their child, and children and parents alike are demonstrating attachment behaviors with one another (spontaneous touch and eye contact, child seeking parent attention positively and looking to parent for safety and reassurance, parent providing positive attention, child demonstrating reciprocal behavior, etc.).

During this phase the therapist wants to be sure that attachment activities are being engaged in outside of the therapy session. The therapy session should not be the only time that the parent and child are engaging in one-on-one focused time together. An adequate support system for the family should be well established. If the attachment between parent and child has been well restored/repaired, the therapist becomes superfluous.

Due to the nature of the therapy, however, parents and children can become attached to the therapist. The child at times can let go more easily than the parent because they are getting their attachment needs met through their parent. It is an important part of the parent work to assist the parent in developing an adequate support system. It may also be useful to taper the ending of therapy by meeting every other week for a period.

5

M-MAT Play: The Frame Part 1

Attachment-based play is the first part of the Multi-Modal Attachment Therapy (M-MAT) parent/child session and, along with M-MAT feeding and questions at the end, creates the frame for the session, framing the talk section in the middle. M-MAT play is implemented in every parent/child session.

What is Attachment-Based Play and Why?

Play has been described as the language of childhood, and so is an ideal vehicle for communicating with children. There are varying definitions of attachment-based play. Attachment-based play is based on the earliest interactions between a parent and child. For the purposes of M-MAT, attachment-based play is interactive and includes one or more of the following elements: touch, eye contact, mirroring and/or singing/rhythm. Think about Peek-A-

Boo, This Little Piggy, clapping games and rhymes and lullabies.

The most important purpose of attachment-based play is for the healing of attachment injuries through the experience of being cared for and engaged. All the talk therapy in the world cannot take the place of the attachment-based play. How many clients, both child and adult, will say they know something in their head, but they don't feel it? By using play, which includes touch, eye contact, mirroring and song and rhythm, with a primary caregiver, the child can have the physical experience of being loved and valued. This replicates the early experiences that support the development of those parts of a young child's brain that are related to attachment and relationship. The therapist is able to engage the non-verbal part of the child's brain through attachment-based play. Combined with the attachment talk therapy and M-MAT feeding and questions, much of the brain is engaged in the healing process through M-MAT.

Attachment-based play serves several functions in the therapy: to encourage appropriate attachment through touch, eye contact, attunement and fun; to give the parents and child a break from the likely negativity in the current relationship, disrupting negative cycles of interaction; and to set the child up to be more receptive to talk portions of therapy by reducing shame and defensiveness.

What attachment-based play is not is board games, imaginative play, competitive games, or intellectual games. Other definitions of attachment-based play may differ from the one provided here. For the purposes of M-MAT the play must include at least one of the four elements: touch, eye contact, mirroring and song/rhythm, and be interactive between caregiver and child. These elements are further described below.

In addition to the activities listed in Appendix A, therapists can find attachment-based play activities online or in other resources. The therapist needs to always evaluate, however, if the activity described meets the criteria for M-MAT attachment-based play before integrating it into the therapy. Appendix A contains a list of attachment-based games that meet M-MAT criteria.

Fun and Play in Attachment

When a child and parent are playing, laughing and having fun together, attachment healing is occurring. Neither child nor parent, at that moment, is in shame. It may take a few sessions for the child and parent to have those moments of fun, but they are priceless.

For the parent who has been struggling with their child every day and every moment, it offers some hope and some positive connection as well. For the child who sees life and relationship as a struggle, and adults, particularly parents, as people to be feared, it begins to create a different story. These moments are essential for healing and creating a new story. The new story is further extended and emphasized through the attachment talk, and the feeding and questions portions of the therapy.

Fun is a theme throughout M-MAT, not only in the play portion, but the talk portion as well. Moments of fun are emphasized and strung together to create a new narrative, and fun with family or caregiver is used as a motivator for the child when appropriate.

Elements of M-MAT Play

Touch

Touch is crucial not only to the development of attachment, but also to overall child development and even survival. Failure to thrive has been linked in some cases to lack of touch, as have poor physical and mental development. One of the first ways an infant interacts with their caregiver is through touch. Parents use touch to sooth, comfort, cuddle and communicate with their babies. Touch is, by definition, connecting. The physical connection through touch is a good metaphor for the emotional connection children need. Attachment injured children have not received adequate touch, and/or have received hurtful touch. It is not unusual for them to avoid touch, or to only use touch in aggressive ways.

Some people may question the use of touch in the therapy session with children who have experienced physical or sexual abuse. These children, more than any, need to know what good, positive, safe touch looks like. They may have no concept of positive touch. It is doing further injury to continue to deprive them of the positive touch they so desperately need.

It is important, however, to be sensitive to the child's response to touch and it is important to create a high level of safety around touch in the session. It is helpful to state very directly to the child and parent that we only use safe, positive touch in session. It not only allows for safety for the child, but also allows the therapist to redirect the child if they become physically aggressive.

Safety is further created by explaining and/or demonstrating with the parent first, asking permission when appropriate, and accepting a child's choice to not participate. It may mean working for a while with very non-threatening touch games such as clapping games. For more intimate activities such as "Gentle touch" (see Appendix A), the therapist has the child and parent play, while the therapist directs or stays out.

The importance of touch for attachment healing cannot be overemphasized. Every M-MAT session should have at least one game that involves touch. Touch is pre-verbal, and since much of attachment injury is preverbal, it can touch and heal the most injured, vulnerable part of the child. Touch can also be encouraged throughout the session as appropriate. For example, a parent can be encouraged to hold or touch a distressed child, or give a high five for a success during a therapeutic conversation.

Eye Contact

Another non-verbal conduit for connecting is eye contact. Think about the times in the supermarket when you have seen a young child with their parent, and the child makes eye contact with you... and just looks at you. They may look down and back up, or look to their parent then back to you. Eye contact precedes verbalizations as a way of connecting. It is common for the attachment injured child to avoid eye contact, or use it only for expressing anger or control. The healthy young child uses eye contact with a parent for safety and reassurance. They will visually check back with a parent in an uncertain or stranger situation.

Eye contact in session is again encouraged through games. Peek-a-boo, eye blink games, and staring contests are some examples (see Appendix A). Eye contact can also be encouraged in the talk portion of the therapy, when appropriate. It should, however, never be forced. Also, the therapist can coach parents to never insist on eye contact when they are angry. The, "YOU LOOK AT ME WHEN I TALK TO YOU!" statement is not useful. The child has to experience eye contact as positive in order to make connecting safe.

Mirroring

Mirroring games help the attunement between parent and child. Parents and infants naturally mirror each other in their interactions and play. In follow the leader/mirroring type games, the parent leads first, then the child. It helps set the hierarchy and gives a chance for the child to follow the parent in a non-oppositional way. The child gets a chance to lead as well, and thus can have the positive experience of being mirrored by an adult.

Singing and Rhythm

Singing and rhythm are regulating, soothing and nurturing. It is one of the classic ways parents communicate comfort and love to their infant. Lullabies are common throughout the world. Rhythm and singing are often integrated into play activities that also utilize touch, eye contact and/or mirroring. Examples include clapping games and Row Row Row Your Boat. Words to well known children's songs can be changed to focus on positive messages to the child. See Appendix A for examples.

Some singing activities are designed specifically to meet the child's need for nurturing. Needless to say, the attachment injured child has generally missed out on a lot of nurturing that occurs in healthier families. Singing, rocking and feeding are all nurturing activities that are included in M-MAT.

Guidelines for Implementing M-MAT Play

In M-MAT, attachment-based play is built into the structure of every parent/child session. It is part of the "Frame" of the session. Attachment based play is engaged in at the very beginning of each and every session, prior to any talk therapy. The second part of the frame, M-MAT feeding and questions, occurs at the end of the session, framing the middle, talk part of the session.

The first thing to do to prepare for the attachment-based play is to get the parents on board. The therapist meets with the parents ahead of time and explains what they will be doing and why. Attachment-based play is generally regressive; that is, the child is allowed to be younger than their physiological age. The therapist explains this to the parents and makes sure they are OK with it. The therapist also tells the parents not to worry if their child does not go along at first. This is to be expected. They do not need to try to make their child participate. The parent and therapist engage in the games with fun and enthusiasm, even if the child does not, periodically encouraging and inviting the child to participate. The therapist asks parents to allow the therapist to handle any behavior in the session, while they work on developing and strengthening the child's attachment.

Sometimes parents are skeptical that their child will want to engage in the attachment based play. They believe their child will feel it is too babyish. That is rarely, if ever, the case. The child is usually quite drawn to the play because it meets a deep inner need.

The therapy supports appropriate hierarchy through the play. The adults are in charge. In any game, the therapist usually goes first, demonstrates, then the parent goes, then the child. The goal is that the child can learn that the adults can be in charge, and it can be both safe and fun!

Therapist → parent → child

While the adults are in charge and the therapist should stay in control of the session, the therapist is not trying to control the child. Ultimately the child needs to be in control of him or herself. This is important. The child choosing to join the play is psychologically very different from the child feeling coerced in some way to participate. Some parents may have difficulty with this, wanting to reward the child after the session if they participate, or consequence them if they do not. This allows the child to manipulate in the session in order to gain the reward or avoid the consequence, then act out later. It is contrary to the M-MAT model.

This response from parents may have to do with the feeling of being out of control. The therapist can emphasize with the parents that they cannot control their child, only control their responses to their child in order to increase or decrease the likelihood of certain behaviors, and that the ultimate goal is for the child to gain self-control. Often, for the attachment injured child, there is nothing the parent can or would want to do that is worse than what they have already experienced. By encouraging the child to participate, but allowing them to not participate, there is no power struggle.

If the child chooses not to participate, the therapist engages in activities with the parent, with enthusiasm, and periodically invites the child in, or, for the withdrawn child, uses the resistance to play peek-a-boo, etc. As long as the child is not doing anything destructive, the therapist stays focused on the activity with the parent, again inviting the child in periodically. The therapist needs to be sure the parent has been prepared ahead of time for this possibility. The child will not want to be left out of the fun for long! There are some activities, like singing to the child, that do not require the child's active participation at all, and these can be easily done as well.

Reasons the child may not participate could be that they are unsure of the safety of the situation, they do not want to give up control, or they are feeling uncomfortable because they are beginning to attach. These first two often happen in the first session. The latter is likely to occur several sessions in, and is actually a sign that the therapy is working. Generally, the child will not hold out for long. Be sure to maintain the structure of the session through periods of avoidance. Do not make the mistake of discontinuing the play due to the child's reluctance.

The therapist uses tools of fun & enthusiasm to engage the child. The child can do no wrong. The therapist stays positive and provides encouraging, nurturing, positive responses even in the face of avoidance or resistance. The main tools of the therapist are enthusiasm and fun.

That being said, limits can and should be set around destructive or aggressive behavior. If a child becomes aggressive, i.e., hitting the parent or being overly rough in the games, it needs to be addressed immediately. The child will more likely be aggressive with the parent rather than the therapist. Using a positive but firm voice tone the therapist can say something like, "Ah ah ah, gentle touch only! Let me show you!" The therapist can then demonstrate, and, if the child allows the therapist to, the therapist can gently take the child's hand and guide it to gently or appropriately touch the parent. As in general good parenting principles the therapist wants to tell the child what they want, rather than focus on what they do not want.

As stated previously, the session should be structured and the structure should be consistent throughout the weeks. This increases predictability and reduces stress and anxiety, making the child more able to participate in and process the therapy.

The therapist should always have the activities planned ahead of time. Indecision creates anxiety for the child and a need to control the situation. A leadership vacuum also creates anxiety for the child and a need to control. Have your activities written down prior to the session and reference this list during the session if needed. If a child asks for a particular activity in the session and it is not on the list, the therapist tells the child that they already have the activities planned for today, but maybe next week they can do it (if it is an appropriate activity). The therapist then puts it on the list for the following week.

This may seem controlling on the part of the therapist, but the therapist is working on letting the child know that the child does not have to be in control all the time (which is exhausting and anxiety producing for the child). The therapist is letting the child know that the adults are in charge and it is OK. The child can relax and be a child. Also, for some children, if they are given this control, they will try to take control of the whole session in a nonproductive way and derail the therapy altogether.

Be aware of what the child and parent may need in the moment. The therapist can alter plans if needed in session based on their own judgement. If the child seems to need a calming activity and the therapist does not have one planned, the therapist can still insert one. Sometimes a parent comes in and is very frustrated with their child, and feels unable to genuinely participate in a more intimate activity, like gentle touch, so the therapist adjusts plans accordingly.

For more complex activities, progress from simple to more complicated, stopping at the level appropriate to the child, thus encouraging success, but adding a little challenge.

Repetition of activities within sessions and across sessions is not only OK, it is very good! The therapist may, for instance, want to start sessions each time with the same clapping game in order to set the routine and provide a level of predictability. The games are very short, and each game can be done about three or four times in the session before moving on to the next game. This allows a chance for mastery, comfort and familiarity with the games.

Some games can be increased in complexity either in the same session, or in subsequent sessions. For instance, the therapist can use the same opening clapping game, but after running through it once or twice in session, if the child and parent have mastered it, the therapist can try it faster with the family, and even faster the time after that, all in a spirit of fun.

Children will benefit from being held and sung to multiple times throughout the course of the therapy. The therapist may only have a few different songs that they use, but they can mix them up and repeat through the course of the therapy. It is useful to repeat singing a short song with the parent to the child three or four times before moving on to the next activity. The therapist should be careful not to become too routine, though, as they may lose engagement with the child. Try to bring in variety as well.

The therapist participates in most games with the parent and child. This helps take some of the pressure off of the parent/child relationship, which is likely already strained, and helps the therapist build rapport with both parent and child. It also allows the parent to feel like they are not in this alone with their child. For children who are very reactive to their parents, the therapist engaging in the games can help act as a buffer, increasing cooperation of the child. It further allows the therapist to demonstrate the activities in a way that can reduce the anxiety, for parent and child, of not knowing what to do, or doing it wrong. More intimate games such as gentle touch or mirrors may be played by parent and child without the therapist, once the therapist has demonstrated, if needed.

Make sure each session has at least one activity involving touch. Touch is the cornerstone of the attachment-based play. It is preferable to have at least one game involving eye contact in a session as well.

In nurturing singing activities, such as "Rock A Bye Baby," it is not expected that child will sing along, although it is fine if they do. This is an opportunity for the adults to provide unconditional nurturing to the child.

Have fun! Stay positive and out of power struggles, utilize resistance, and have fun! Fun increases bonding and reduces shame. When a child is having fun the child is not in shame, which allows them to be better able to connect with their caregiver and also allows them to better participate later in the talk portion of the session.

Keep a positive tone of voice. This is very important. Children will respond to tone of voice before they respond to words. The therapist's voice tone should convey enthusiasm and fun! To see what this looks like, observe or imagine a well trained, experienced preschool teacher. Note the positive tone of voice the teacher uses to corral the children into circle time: "OK, It's circle time! Come sit on your mats!" Enthusiasm is conveyed and the children are more likely to pay attention and comply.

Direct, do not ask the child. Asking the child if they want to participate sets the therapist up for a "no" answer, which will ultimately make it harder for the child to participate. The skilled preschool teacher imagined above does not ask the children to come sit on their mats, she does not plead, she directs them, but with such a positive voice tone that resistance is reduced. Similarly, in session, the therapist directs, but with positivity. The therapist does not make the mistake of asking the child if they want, for instance, to play a clapping game. Instead, the therapist

Do not ask, tell

says with enthusiasm something like, "We're going start today with a clapping game! It goes like this..."

Do not try to verbally process the attachment-based play. The play is experiential, and designed to address preverbal injuries. Trying to verbally process the play may move the child into an older state and out of the experience, and it may also increase resistance.

Be patient and expect resistance. The more disturbed the attachment, the longer it may take for the child to relinquish control. It is not unusual for a child to go along at first, but then to go through a period of avoidance. This is a signal that the child is getting too close for comfort, and is a last-ditch effort to maintain distance and/or control. This is a sign of progress. Stay consistent and positive. This phase does not usually last long.

Reflect after each session what worked and what didn't. What type of activities does the child most need at this time in the therapy? Does the child need to start the session with a more regulating activity? Does the child need more focus on nurture? Consider each session as feedback for planning the next session.

To sum up the guidelines for implementing attachment-based play in M-MAT:

1. Attachment-based play is a part of every session.
2. Get the parents on board.
3. Establish hierarchy.
4. There is no attempt to control the child.
5. The child can choose to not participate - Parent and therapist continue with the play inviting child in regularly.
6. The therapist uses tools of fun & enthusiasm to engage the child.
7. The child can do no wrong.
8. Set limits around aggression.

9. The session should be structured and the structure consistent across sessions.
10. Always have activities planned ahead of time.
11. Be sensitive to parent and child needs in the moment, adjusting activities if needed.
12. For more complex activities, progress from simple to more complicated, stopping at the level appropriate to the child.
13. Repetition of activities within sessions and across sessions is not only OK, it can be very good!
14. The therapist participates in most games.
15. More intimate games such as gentle touch may be played by parent and child without the therapist (once the therapist has demonstrated if needed).
16. Each session should have at least one game involving touch and one with eye contact.
17. Nurturing activities such as singing do not have any expectation of the child's active participation.
18. Have Fun!
19. Keep a positive tone of voice.
20. Direct, don't ask.
21. Do not try to verbally process attachment-based play.
22. Be patient and expect resistance.
23. Reflect after each session what worked and what didn't and plan the next session accordingly.

What To Do When...

• Child refuses to play - That is OK. Play the games with the parent, in a spirit of fun, and with enthusiasm. Prepare the parent well in advance of the parent/child sessions that this may happen, and that it is OK and that the therapist and parent will continue to play games with one another, while periodically inviting the child in.

Ignore any distracting behavior by the child, but continue to invite them to play. Usually children will not sit out for too long, because they do not want to be left out. Remember, fun and enthusiasm are the M-MAT therapist's tools for engagement!

- Child becomes overly agitated/excited in the play - Integrate more regulating/self-calming games such as rhythm games and breathing games. Also stop/go games (like Fast/Slow clapping in Appendix A) help a child to learn to regulate after excitement. Do some quiet singing games with the parent holding and rocking the child at the end of the play portion to help them regulate. The therapist may find the child gets overactive standing up, so the therapist may choose only sitting games for a while until the child has learned to regulate their energy level better. Use each session to plan the next session in determining what works best for the child. If a game seems too activating for the child, move on to the next game.

- Child becomes aggressive in the play - Remind the child, "Gentle touch! We only use gentle touch in here." Physically and gently redirect the child to gentle touch if needed, and as the child will allow. Usually if the child becomes aggressive it will be with the parent. Often the child will allow the therapist to take their hand and physically demonstrate gentle touch with the parent using the child's hand, saying something like, "We touch gentle, like this". Early on in the therapy, the therapist should talk about using only gentle and safe touch in the session.

- Child becomes inappropriately physically affectionate with therapist - This is a good opportunity to teach boundaries around touch. For example, if a child jumps into the therapist's lap, the therapist can gently remove them and say something like, "Oh, you know, we don't know each other very well. When you don't know someone very well, you can give them a hand shake, like this..." (demonstrate). The therapist might ask the parent, "Whose lap is it OK for (child) to sit on?" Parents, maybe grandparents might be identified. The therapist can then engage child and parent in a short conversation around this.

- Child is inappropriate in touch with caregiver - For instance, a child starts kissing a caregiver's neck in a way that feels inappropriate. This can happen particularly with sexually abused children. Again with a positive voice tone, limits are set, parents are asked to tell the child what would be an appropriate way to touch them (i.e., a hug or a high five). Some children hug in a way that does not feel appropriate, holding on too long or too tightly. Sometimes the hug can feel controlling. In this case it is good to teach an appropriate hug, i.e., ask for the hug, then hug for a count of 4 or 5, then release. This can be done briefly in the moment. If there is a persistent problem it can be further addressed in the talk/skills building section of the therapy.

- Child is highly reactive to touch - Slow down, ask permission to touch. Give the child the option to opt out of touch. Again, continue with the parent, modeling and demonstrating the safety of the activity. Start with less intense types of touch games like clapping games and high fives. See if the child prefers firm or light touch. Consider the possibility of sensory integration issues and refer to an occupational therapist specializing in sensory integration if appropriate. Also be sure that autism spectrum disorders have been ruled out.

6

M-MAT Feeding and Questions: The Frame Part 2

M-MAT Feeding and Questions is the third and last part of the Multi-Modal Attachment Therapy (M-MAT) session. It is the second part of the frame and, along with attachment-based play at the beginning, frames the talk section in the middle. M-MAT Feeding and Questions is implemented in every parent/child therapy session.

What are Feeding and Attachment Questions and Why?

Feeding is a fundamental part of caring for young children. In M-MAT it represents nurturing and the parent's ability to take care of the child's needs. It also engages more of the child's senses in the therapeutic process. Taste and smell are inextricably linked to early memories. By using feeding we are able to engage yet another part of the child's brain in the therapy. Feeding is also soothing and grounding, supporting the child in leaving the session in a well regulated state.

In M-MAT the feeding ritual is tied to attachment questions. These attachment questions are based on the idea of "stringing pearls" from Narrative Therapy. The idea is to identify discreet moments (pearls) and to string them together to support an alternative narrative to the dominant, oppressive narrative. Attachment questions are designed to support the attachment between child and caregiver.

Each week, at the end of the session, the therapist asks about positive experiences and appreciations between parent and child, past, present and future, creating a new story or narrative. The narrative that the therapist is working to develop and support is that the parent enjoys and values their child, and the parent/child relationship can be fun and positive. These questions are asked at the end of the session as part of a feeding ritual, and, thus, the session always ends on a positive note.

Attachment Questions

Sample attachment questions include:

> What is a time that you remember having fun with Suzie when she was just a little girl?
> Suzie, can you remember a time when you had fun with your (mother or family)?
> What is a time recently that you and Suzie had fun?
> Can you think of a time this week that you two had fun together?
> What is something you look forward to doing with Suzie?

Suzie, what is something you look forward to doing with your mom?

What is something you appreciate about Suzie?

Suzie, what is something you appreciate about your mom?

What is one thing Suzie did for you this week?

What is one thing your mom did for you this week?

Mom, how about when Suzie is a bit older, maybe a teenager or even adult, what is something you look forward to doing with her?

Suzie, what is something you look forward to doing with your mom when you are a lot older?

The therapist is also trying to re-story the idea that the parent does not care about the child. Children often have no idea or awareness of all that their parents do for them as a matter of course, and attachment injured children may be particularly blind to this. The following questions are useful in addressing this:

Mom, what is something that you do to show Johnny that you care about him?

Johnny, what is something you think your mom does that shows she cares about you?

Moms do a lot of things for their kids and most of the time we don't even notice! Mom, what is one thing you do for Johnny?

Johnny, what is one thing your mom does for you regularly?

It is also good to define coming to therapy as something the parent does for the child:

And I know something else she does for you! She brings you here every week and works together with us!

Process   answer → feed (cracker)

In M-MAT feeding and questions, questions are asked alternating between parent and child. The parent answers the question first, then the child. This allows the parent to model for the child, and to verbally give to the child first. Each time a question is answered, the parent feeds the child a small snack. The snack is agreed to ahead of time by the parent, making sure that it is something the child likes. Small tasty crackers tend to work quite well. Parents sometimes playfully fly or swim the little crackers or snacks into their child's mouth. The child's boundaries are always respected, however, and some children may not be comfortable with this. They may, for instance, prefer to have their parent put the snack in their hand, and that is fine.

At some point in the therapy, the child will often want to feed the parent as well. This is likely either due to the child wanting to reciprocate, which is a positive sign of progress, or it is because the child wants more control. Either way, if this works for the parent, then the feeding alternates between parent and child, with the parent always feeding the child first (maintaining an appropriate hierarchy).

Child feeding parent ok →

Repetition. Repetition. Repetition. Repetition of questions week to week is OK and desirable. For instance, most weeks the therapist should ask about a time the parent and child had fun together that week. Sometimes they may have a hard time remembering a time that week, and if the therapist noticed them having fun in the session, perhaps during the attachment-based play, the therapist can suggest that as a possibility. Other times the therapist can extend the timeline to, "How about any time in the past?" It is only necessary to do three or four questions per session. The repetition over the weeks is enough to make an impression and the snack/feeding is symbolic.

Sometimes the child has a hard time coming up with answers. It is OK, then, to focus on asking questions only of the parent while they feed the child. As with infants, the focus is on the parent nurturing and feeding the child, both literally and figuratively. It is likely that as the therapy progresses, the child will better be able to participate in answering questions.

Every parent/child session ends with this ritual. It usually only takes a few minutes, and the session always ends on a positive note. Thus, each parent/child session is framed by the attachment-based play at the beginning, and the feeding and attachment questions at the end. This frame creates a therapeutic container for the talk section in the middle.

3-4 questions

7

M-MAT Talk

Multi-Modal Attachment Therapy (M-MAT) Talk occurs in the middle of the therapy session, framed by the attachment-based play at the beginning and the feeding and attachment questions at the end.

What is Attachment Talk and Why?

While attachment-based play is largely non-verbal and experiential, the attachment talk therapy engages the thinking, verbal part of the brain. Thus, by integrating both attachment-based play and attachment talk therapy, M-MAT attempts to treat the whole child, endeavoring to engage as much of the brain as possible in healing.

The talk portion of M-MAT can be divided into four different categories: Re-Storying, Skill Building, Psychoeducation and Addressing Behavior. Throughout all of the talk therapy, the therapist is always trying to speak in a way that supports a new, healthier narrative for the child: that the child is valuable and loved and cared for.

Much attachment injury occurs pre-verbally for the child, but the child has grown and with that growth is the incredible cognitive growth that occurs during early childhood. Unfortunately, for the attachment injured child, much of that growth has occurred around a faulty template of how the world works, based on the child's early experiences. Maladaptive beliefs become the filters through which the child views the world, and around which cognitive development is organized. These beliefs are tied to the child's survival, so are held tightly, though often not consciously. The Re-Storying part of the attachment talk addresses these faulty beliefs head on.

Research is also clear that early neglect and abuse cause deficits in the child's functioning and cognition, including difficulty self-soothing, identifying and expressing emotion, deficits in cause and effect reasoning, and social difficulties. Skill deficits are addressed through skill building talk, games and exercises.

Psychoeducation is used throughout the talk portion of M-MAT, but there are a few areas the therapist will want to address specifically: healthy shame vs guilt and parent/ child roles and clarifying responsibility. Opportunities to address these issues may come up naturally in session or the therapist may plan to address them specifically.

Also, due to the maladaptive beliefs and skill deficits, the child is likely exhibiting behavior problems. It is often these behavioral difficulties that have brought the child in to therapy in the first place. The child's maladaptive beliefs and skill deficits can both generate a lot of behavior problems, and also interfere with the ability of the parents to be effective in addressing those behaviors. A negative spiral can occur in the interactions between parent and child as the parent tries to address the child's behavior.

The Addressing Behavior portion of the attachment talk is geared at disrupting that negative cycle, helping the child to understand discipline differently, and providing the parent with additional parenting tools.

Specific interventions in each of the four categories (re-storying, skill building, psychoeducation and addressing behaviors) are described below. How to integrate these into the therapy over time is further clarified in Chapter 9: Putting It All Together, including a sample therapy timeline.

Re-Storying

Many of the ideas for re-storying derive from Narrative Therapy concepts. The idea is that the child has created a story line for their life based on the child's interpretation of events. This story line then invests new events with the same meanings and themes of the maladaptive or dominant story line. Any events that do not fit into the original or dominant story line are often simply not seen or noticed. For instance, a child who was abused or neglected when young may have created a story line that goes something like: I was a bad kid so people hurt me and no one loved me; I am still bad so no one will ever love me, they will only hurt me. These themes or story lines are often not conscious for the child, and yet the child acts from that perspective. One can see how this story line or theme would create difficulties for the child attaching to a caregiver.

It is also easy to see how this child might become easily dysregulated because the child sees themselves as bad, which creates intolerable feelings of shame and anxiety. It does not take much to trigger these difficult feelings (shame, hurt, anger) and push the child over their ability to cope. Contributing to this is the fact the child's coping/self-soothing skills are often minimal due to their early history.

Furthermore, if a child feels they are bad, they will do bad things, even when not dysregulated, creating a lot of discipline challenges. Then, if a caregiver tries to discipline the child, the child will interpret it as, "I'm bad" and, "they are trying to hurt me (with the discipline)." It will be very difficult for the child to see that the caregiver is trying to help them through discipline or consequences and so there develops a vicious cycle.

The underlying dominant, maladaptive story must be addressed early in the therapy in order to effectively do any other work.

The goal then of the Re-Storying talk portion is to help the child re-write their story. In the talk portion of M-MAT, this is done primarily through the Story of Love, the Attachment Narrative, What Do Babies Need, and the Heart of Hearts interventions as described below. The stringing pearls concept discussed in Chapter 6: Feeding and Questions, is also part of the re-storying for the child, as are the experiences in the attachment based play.

Story of Love

The Story of Love is the first talk portion of M-MAT that the therapist engages the child and parent in. Remember, the talk portion is sandwiched between the attachment-based play, and the feeding and questions portions of the session. The story of love should be the only topic of the talk portion in this session. This first talk session will start with attachment-based play, move on to the story of love, and end with feeding and attachment questions. This may be a short session, under the standard 50 minutes, which is fine.

There is a great deal of power in speaking about love, yet as therapists, we do not often do it. In telling the story of love, the therapist, with the parent, is defining the love of parent to child as unconditional and ever present, everlasting. The story of love is told from the past, to the present, to the future.

This story is told as a conversation between parent and therapist with the child in the room. Nothing is expected of the child. It is good to encourage the child to sit with the parent, but if they don't, it is OK as this hypervigilant child will be listening to every word. The child can sit with the parent, wander around the room, fidget with a toy. The fact that nothing is expected or demanded of the child during this intervention is important, because it reduces the child's anxiety, which will allow them to absorb the information better.

It is also good to brief the parent ahead of time, but this intervention can usually be accomplished successfully without the parent having prior knowledge. A reasonably healthy parent will be able to answer these questions appropriately. If the parent is unable to answer these questions appropriately, then that is a sign that the parent is not ready to participate in M-MAT.

The therapist both prompts the discussion with questions, and highlights the desired answer by repeating/ reflecting what the parent says. The repeating/reflecting is important because it allows the child to hear the information not only from a parent, against whom the child may have a lot of defenses, but from the therapist as well. Repetition is also important as one tool in getting the new story, new information through to the child. The following is an example. Of course the timeline will vary depending on whether the therapist is speaking to bio parents or adoptive parents or relative caregivers, and parent answers will vary, but the idea is the same. The

therapist should use a leisurely pace in their speech and
not run through the questions too quickly:

Therapist: (to parent) So I'm just wondering, how much
you love Johnny? Do you love him this much (hands close
together), this much (hands further apart), or this much
(hands and arms spread far apart)?

Parent: Parent will often say something like "I love him to
the moon and back!" or "more than my arms can stretch"
or "this far" (stretching their arms as far as they can).

Therapist: Oh, you love him...(repeating what parent
said).

Parent: Yes!

Therapist: OK, when did you start loving Johnny? When
is the first time you felt that love for him?

Parent: When I first saw his face, I just fell in love with
him. I knew he was my boy!

Therapist: Ah, so when you first saw his face, you just fell
in love with him. You knew that he was your little boy!

Parent: confirms

Therapist: OK, so you first loved him when you first saw
his beautiful face, but, you know, when children are
toddlers, 2 or 3 years old, they can be so active, running
around, getting into everything! Did you still love him
then?

Parent: affirms

Therapist: Ok, you loved him when you first saw his face,
and, when he was a toddler, running around getting into
everything, you still loved him. How about now? Now that
Johnny is 6 years old, do you still love him?

Parent: affirms

Therapist: OK, so you loved him in the past, and you love
him now, but what about when Johnny is 10 years old, do
you think you will love him then?

Parent: Of Course! I'll always love him!

Therapist: Of Course! You'll always love him! OK, OK, I hear you, but you know teenagers can be a little difficult. When he is a teenager, maybe wearing funny clothes or getting his hair cut funny, do you think you will still love him?

Parent: affirmation

Therapist: Are you sure?

Parent: affirmation

Therapist: OK, so you loved him when you first saw his face, you loved him when he was little, you love him now, and you'll even love him when he is a teenager. But, what about when he is a grown up? When Johnny grows up and maybe moves out of the house and is an adult, say, 22 years old, will you still love him then?

Parent: affirmation

Therapist: OK, and if Johnny grows up and should decide to have children, and he may or may not, but if he does, that mean his children will be...?

Parent: my grandchildren...

Therapist Ohhh... so that means you...would be... his children's grandma? (this seems particularly helpful for children who are adopted as it fully confirms them as part of the family).

Parent: affirmation

Therapist: When do you think you will stop loving Johnny?

Parent: Never!

Therapist: Are you sure?

Parent: affirmation

Therapist: Does that mean that you will always love Johnny?

Parent: affirmation

Therapist: Forever and ever?

Parent: affirmation

Therapist: No matter what?

Parent: I will always love Johnny no matter what
Therapist: Wow, you'll always love Johnny no matter what. I am hearing that you will always, always love him.
Parent: affirms
Therapist: OK, well that is good to know. Thanks for letting me know that. Let's move on to the last part of our time together today...

All the while, the child is listening. This is followed by the M-MAT feeding and questions part of the session.

This one session is not likely enough to convince the child that they are loved, or to change their narrative, but the Story of Love, combined with attachment-based play and feeding and questions, is a good beginning!

Attachment Narrative - The Child's Story

The attachment narrative is perhaps the single most important intervention in the talk portion of M-MAT. It forms the core upon which the child's new story develops. The attachment narrative is a re-telling of the child's story from birth to present. The therapist, parent, and child revisit all the child's important life events. The therapist and parent help the child make sense of their story and correct cognitive distortions or misunderstandings of the meanings of the events. Along the way, new meanings are created.

The child may actively participate in the telling or not, depending on age and the child's readiness and ability to participate. Most children will participate at least a little in the telling of their story, but there is no pressure to do so. They can be invited, but not required.

Be clear that the Attachment Narrative is not the same as the trauma narrative in TF-CBT (Trauma Focused Cognitive Behavioral Therapy). The trauma narrative in

TF-CBT focuses specifically on trauma and processing trauma, going into a lot of specific detail regarding a traumatic event. The attachment narrative takes a much wider view, reviewing the whole life of the child from birth. The attachment narrative recounts both difficult and positive events in the child's life. Any trauma the child has experienced is discussed in the attachment narrative in the context of the child's life, but in a much more general way. The details are not explored, but the meaning of any such event is.

Going into the details of trauma is not necessary in M-MAT and can trigger PTSD symptoms or re-traumatize the child. It is the meaning the child has made of the trauma that is causing the child the most difficulty in their life. This is what is focused on and addressed in the attachment narrative.

The attachment narrative is done before skill building interventions because the child is not likely to be cooperative with skill building early in the therapy. The issues discussed in the attachment narrative are already present for the child and the attachment narrative often provides the child with some relief. As stated, details of trauma are not explored, as it is not necessary, and this helps avoid re-traumatizing the child. How events are addressed will become more evident in the example below.

The attachment narrative, or child's story, is told during the talk portion of the therapy session, after the attachment-based play and before the feeding and attachment questions. The attachment-based play, along with the feeding and questions, constitute the frame of the therapy session, which provides a therapeutic container for the talk portion. This promotes soothing and regulating for the child, and ensures that the session ends on a positive note.

The child needs to make sense of their experiences. It is OK to use leading questions to direct the conversation. The therapist uses questions and comments and reflection to highlight and enhance particular aspects of the story in a way that creates a healthier story line or theme.

The therapist works with the parent and child to tell the child's story from birth on, including both positive events and stories about the child, and traumas and other events (i.e., separations) that could disrupt attachment. The therapist leads the discussion of feelings associated with the event for both parent and child. The therapist and parent correct errors in thinking and clarify responsibility and fault throughout. The therapist elicits apology from parent to child for not protecting child as each trauma is discussed, or for other attachment disrupting behavior, such as parental substance abuse. The therapist facilitates the conversation about how things are different (safer, better) now.

The therapist should cover:

- Child is not at fault - Children carry a lot of shame and responsibility for their parent's poor behavior. They feel that they are bad or these things would not have happened to them. This is a core belief that needs to be addressed both directly and indirectly.
- Empathy and normalization for Child's feelings - The child may not be able to express their feelings. It is OK to say things like: "That could be so hard for a little kid" or, "Gosh, that must have been so confusing."
- Apology parent to child - Even if the parent is not the one responsible for the neglect or abuse (such as an adoptive parent), this is important. This removes the shame from the child and reinforces the idea that the child is not at fault. All children deserve to be well loved and cared for and protected. The apology acknowledges this, and holds

the adults accountable. This supports healing for the child. An example of how to do this with an adoptive parent is given below.

- How the parent has tried or is trying to help and support the child - The child is often quite oblivious to the ways in which the parent has been there for them or has tried to support them. It does not fit with their dominant maladaptive story, so parents' protective or supportive behavior is misinterpreted or not seen at all.
- Why things are different now/why child is safe now; includes parent, child, and situational changes - This helps reduce anxiety and changes the present story to "I am safe" from "I am not safe."
- What the child can do if the child ever feels unsafe - Included in this should be going to the parent and/or other supportive adults. The child may not know how to do this as it may not have been an option in their early experience. This changes the story from "I'm on my own, no one can help me" to "I can get help, I have grown ups in my life who will help and protect me." It is also empowering for the child to have some concrete strategies that move them from the powerless infant place to a place of power.

The adults are responsible for clarifying the story. The child participates as able. The therapist can support the parent in providing nurturing during the narrative, i.e., holding, hugs, rubbing the child's back, as needed and appropriate and as the child will allow.

Some of the tools used during the narrative are:

- Repetition and reflection to highlight desired points (corrected cognitions).
- Psychoeducation.
- Having parent verbally reinforce corrected cognitions.

• Bringing in child's experience of babies/young children to explore ideas around responsibility.

The therapist should talk to the parent ahead of time about the attachment narrative. It is important that parents know that both difficult and positive things will be talked about so they are psychologically prepared. Explain the rationale for the attachment narrative. Explain the process. Let them know that the therapist will be asking questions and highlighting events and answers, but they should feel free to add anything they feel is important.

Introduce the attachment narrative in the session with parent and child as the child's story. For a child who is able and willing to participate, the conversation moves between parent and child, as each is able to fill in relevant parts of the child's story. Start with where the child was born. The therapist can ask the child this question first, then default to the parent if the child cannot answer or does not know. This gives an easily defined, objective starting point to the child's story. While the child's story starts well before they were born with the family history and pregnancy, it is sufficient for the purpose of the attachment narrative to start with the birth of the child. The below example gives some of the therapist's questions and cues for an adopted child with her adoptive mother:

• Introduce the topic:

> Today we are going to tell the story of Sarah!
> Sarah, do you know where you were born?....Oh, you were born in San Antonio!
> Now you would have been too young to remember anything about your birth, but have you ever heard any stories about the day you were born?...
> No?...

Mom, do you know anything about Sarah's birth?...
Was she born in a hospital?...
Do you know, after she was born, where she went home to?...Who was in the home that she went home to?...
OK, so after she was born she went home with her mother to her grandmother's house.

- Include positives such as:

  I bet you were a cute baby! Mom, do you have any pictures of Sarah when she was a baby?...Sarah and Mom, do you know any stories from when Sarah was just little?

- Introduce difficult subjects:

  I know some hard things happened when you were still very little. Mom, what were some of the hard things that happened when Sarah was little...Sarah, what do you remember about what happened?

- Give the opportunity for sharing of information (may be documented in court or child welfare documents).

  ...Oh, so Sarah's bio mom and bio-grandma both struggled with addiction... (discuss difficulties the biological parent may have had that affected the child, but never put down biological parents. To attack the biological parent is to attack the child).

- Provide psychoeducation:

  ...Gosh, when parents are struggling with addiction they usually have a really hard time providing their babies with what they need...that can be so hard for the babies (empathy)...

When Babies or little kids don't get what they need, they can be so sad and angry and confused. Sometimes they even think that it's their fault!

- Provide more psychoeducation and correct the presumed cognitive distortions:

    ...It is a funny thing, the way little kids' brains work, they think whenever something hard or bad happens it is their fault, but you know, it is never the baby's or kid's fault. Never, ever! Babies are just babies that need and deserve to be taken care of and loved and protected.

- Have the parent reinforce the correction:

    Sometimes kids think if they were just better kids or better babies their bio mom might have been able to care for them better or not done drugs in the first place. Mom, do you think it is in any way Sarah's fault that her bio mom wasn't able to take good care of her?...Or did drugs?...
    That's right, it is never the child's fault!

- Bring in the child's experience of younger children/ babies.

    Sarah, do you know any one-year-olds?...Do they cry sometimes?...Is it OK if they cry or fuss or get into things?...
    That is right, that is just what little kids do!
    Would it ever be OK to hurt (name of child Sarah knows)?

Of course not! She is just a baby!

What if the grown-ups around her were having problems and didn't take care of her right? Would it ever be her fault?

Of course not! Grown-ups are responsible for their own behavior! Babies and little kids are just babies and little kids! They are never responsible for a grown-up's behavior!

- Move towards an apology parent to child, even with an adoptive parent who was not there at the time:

  Mom, I know how much you love Sarah. You must feel so bad that she was not cared for right when she was little...(give a chance for parent's response).

  You know even when it is not our fault, when we weren't there, as parents we feel so bad when our children get hurt. I bet you wish you could have been there, that you could have made sure Sarah was cared for like she deserved to be! (space for parent response).

  Can you look at Sarah and tell her how sorry you are that she was not well cared for when she was just little...that you weren't able to be there for her?

  Parent: Sarah, I am so sorry you weren't cared for right when you were little. I wish I had known you then. I wish I could have been there for you and kept you safe.

- The therapist might prompt the parent to give Sarah a hug at this point, if the parent isn't already doing so, and it feels appropriate:

  Mom, do you want to give Sarah a hug?

- Focus on how things are different/better now. Talking about difficult things has likely raised the child's anxiety. This not only continues to create a new story, but also reduces the child's anxiety:

  How are things different now than they were when you were a baby?

- Repeat, reflect and highlight the answers that are part of the new story:

  That's right, you are older and bigger now! You can get help if you need to!
  Mom, how are things different/safer now than when Sarah was a baby?

- Again, repeat, reflect and highlight the answers that are part of the new story:

  That's right, you are able to take care of Sarah. You don't do drugs, and you always make sure Sarah has food to eat and a safe place to sleep. You are able to take care of Sarah!

After some further elaboration on how things are different now, this may be a good stopping point for this talk part of this session. The attachment narrative can be told in pieces over a number of sessions. The therapist wants to be sure to end each talk portion on a positive note. The therapist can now move the session to the feeding and questions:

  Well, I think we have talked enough for today! We'll keep telling Sarah's story next time we meet. Let's move on to our snack.

The feeding and questions portion is positive, grounding and soothing, preparing the child to re-enter the world. In the next session, the attachment narrative will pick up where it left off in the timeline of the child's life.

Throughout the attachment narrative, the therapist also focuses on, highlights and expands the elements that support a new and positive understanding of the role of the parent in the child's life. For instance, when working with a mother and child, if part of a story is that the mother called the police when she found out that abuse was occurring, the therapist would highlight this protective act on the mother's part by asking questions and inquiring further about the meaning of this. For instance, the therapist might say:

So you mean that as soon as you found out, you called the police?
How come you called the police when you found out?
That's right, it is illegal for an adult to hurt a child!...
People understand that it is the grown-ups who are responsible when something like this happens. The grown-ups know better, and children are just children and should not be hurt. That's why it is illegal for grown-ups to hurt children (psychoeducation).
So, Mom, you must have known that it was not Sam's fault...
And why else did you call the police?
Oh, so you did not want Sam to be hurt any more...
You wanted to keep him safe...
That's right, you wanted to protect him...
And why did you want to protect him?...Of course, because you love him and never want to see him hurt. Sam deserves to be safe and protected...

This, then, is a good opportunity to explore the mother's feelings and move towards an apology:

> You know, when something like this happens, moms usually feel pretty bad that they had not been able to keep it from happening. I bet you feel pretty bad that this happened to your little boy...
> That's right...so even though you did not mean for this to happen, and it wasn't your fault, can you let Sam know how sorry you are that (name of perpetrator) hurt him; that you couldn't protect him? Can you look at Johnny and tell him how sorry you are?
> **Parent:** I am so sorry that you were hurt. I'm so sorry that I wasn't able to keep him from hurting you.

Highlight again the protective act:

> But when you did find out, you were able to protect Sam. When you called the police, you were protecting him.

The therapist now moves on to "how things are different now". Asking questions on why the child is safer now, and elaborating. These should include:

• How circumstances have changed.
• How the parent is keeping the child safe.
• How the child can help keep themselves safe.
• What child can do if they ever feel unsafe.

The attachment narrative is continued every week in a linear timeline until the child's story is told up to the child's current age. The child is encouraged to ask questions of the parent as the story is told. The following life events should be included:

- Child's birth
- Who the child lived with
- Positives about the child
- Changes in living situation
- Birth of sibling(s)
- Trauma and neglect

In regards to siblings, there is sometimes a theme or distorted cognition that there is not enough love in the family to go around, or a sibling is more loved than the child. If this seems to be the case, it can be addressed during the narrative with questions such as these:

You know, sometimes kids think that their parents don't have enough love for all of their children. Mom, do you have enough love in your heart for both of your children?
Are you sure?
If you love Billy are you able to love Sam as well?

Sometimes, particularly with older children, there will be a need to revisit events that were not fully explored initially or that the child has further questions about.

It is not unusual for parents or caregivers to become emotional or tearful during the attachment narrative, particularly when discussing emotional issues such as their child's early abuse or neglect. This is an excellent opportunity for modeling of appropriate emotional expression, and reassuring the child of their parent's emotional strength. It is also a good opportunity to reinforce the parent's caring for their child. Through their parent's modeling, children can learn that it is OK to be sad, and OK to express emotion.

Children may feel overwhelmed in the face of their parents' emotions and may feel they need to take care of the parent. The therapist lets the child know that it is OK to feel, and that their parent is strong and can handle their feelings. The therapist:

• Acknowledges the emotion — *Parent's*
• Acknowledges how the child may be feeling in the face of that emotion.
• Expresses why, as a therapist, they are not worried about the parent.
• Has the parent express to the child that they are OK.
• Explores the meaning of the emotion, tying it into the parent's caring for the child and other M-MAT talk themes.

This would look something like this:

Therapist: I see, Mom, that you are getting emotional. You know sometimes when kids see their parents get emotional they are worried that their parents are not OK. I know, though, that you are OK. I know that you can feel strong emotions and still be OK.
Therapist: (To child) I'm not worried about your mom because I know how strong she is and I know it is OK to have feelings, and that your mom is OK.
Therapist: (to Mom) Mom, what are you feeling?
Mom: I'm feeling sad.
Therapist: Oh, you are feeling sad. Can you let Maria know that even though you feel sad, you are OK?
Mom: Maria, I feel sad, but I'm OK.
Therapist: Can you tell Maria why you are feeling sad? What is sad for you?

Mom: I'm sad that things were so hard for you when you were little. I wish no one had ever hurt you. I wish I could have been there for you then.

Therapist: (reflecting) You wish no one had ever hurt your little girl. You wish you could have been there for her.

From here the therapist can explore with parent and child the M-MAT themes of fault and guilt (not the child's fault), parent's caring for the child, apology parent to child, and/or how things are different now.

If the child tends to do a lot of self-blaming, it may be important as well to have the parent reassure the child that it is not the child's fault that the parent is sad. The child is not responsible for the parent's emotions.

If the parent has some responsibility for what occurred to the child, then this is a good time to move to an apology from parent to child. This is therapeutic for both parent and child.

What Do Babies Need?

This is a helpful intervention when the child is in a new home setting, such as an adoptive home. It helps both child and parent to understand why the child is having such a hard time trusting and accepting love and support from their new parents or caregivers, and also explores the idea that the new situation is different from the old situation, supporting a new story for the child.

The therapist pulls out a baby doll to illustrate. The following are some of the questions and psychoeducation that the therapist provides. The questions are asked of the child with the parent providing support:

Here is a baby, what do you think babies need?
That's right, they need food and they need a home.

What else do they need?

Do you think babies need love?

How do you think people show their babies they love them?

That's right, they take care of them. They change their diapers and hold them when they cry, they make sure they are fed, and they play with them.

Did you know that babies, to be healthy and happy, need to be held and touched?

That is one of the ways parents let their babies know that they love them, even before the baby can understand their words, they hold and hug their babies in good gentle ways.

Babies don't have words yet, so how do babies let their parents know that they need something?

Is it OK for a baby to cry?

Yes, of course it is OK – that is the way they let their parents know they don't feel good.

When a baby cries, and their parent picks them up and takes care of them, the baby learns that they can trust their parent. The baby learns that their parent is there for them.

For inhibited attachment: When that doesn't happen, the baby is not sure if they can trust grown-ups, and sometimes doesn't think that any grown-ups can really help them.

For disinhibited attachment: When that doesn't happen, the baby might start to look to any and everyone, even strangers, to get what they need. They don't know what it is like to have a special person, a parent, really take care of them.

So how are things different now? Do you think (your adoptive parents) can take care of you?

How do they take care of you?...

(To parent) What are some of the ways that you take care of Michael?

What are some of the other things you do for him?

That's right, you...And, another thing I know you do for him is to bring him here and meet with me and Michael.

So your mom is different than your bio mom was. What other ways is she different?

Does she do drugs (if the bio parents did drugs)?... (Sometimes the child will express a concern here that, for instance, their adoptive mom has a glass of wine at night. It is important to explore these concerns with child and parent and how it is different and to allay fears.)

This intervention is ended with how things are different now.

Heart of Hearts

This is a strategy that can be used as needed throughout the therapy. In trying to help the child re-write their story, the therapist and parent are trying to communicate that there is a valuable, amazing child underneath the lies of the dominant or dysfunctional story. We can speak directly to that inner healthy child. If used sparingly and appropriately, children generally do not balk at this because it does resonate with their inner needs. The therapist wants to be careful not to use this as a way to negate the child's experience. The therapist can do this in part by being tentative and owning the idea through "I think..." statements, and not using it as a direct contradiction to something the child just said.

For instance, the therapist and parent, in the presence of the child, may be discussing how the parent would love to have the child fully engaged with the family and be able to have good relationships with everyone in the family. The therapist might say, "You know, I think, in his heart of hearts, Sam wants that too. I believe, in his heart of hearts, Sam wants to be part of the family, wants to have a good relationship with everyone."

It is important that the therapist does not require the child to state this or confirm this, because that sets the child up for a "no" response, and an argument or power struggle over the issue, further entrenching the child in an opposite view. The therapist just makes the statement and moves on.

Skill Building

The skill building portion of M-MAT is largely the same as in other child therapies involving skill building activities. Skill building activities may include games, role play and discussion. Do not confuse skill building games with attachment-based play, however. The parameters, focus, and methods are different. Skill building falls into the talk portion of M-MAT, occurring in the middle of the therapy session, framed by the attachment-based play, and the feeding and questions sections.

In the course of the therapy, skill building should occur after the story of love and attachment narrative, and once the child is somewhat cooperative in the session. If the therapist tries working on skill building too early, there is a good chance that the child will not cooperate or will be too anxious to fully absorb the information or to participate fully.

Four areas of skill building that should always be included with attachment injured children are self-regulation/self-soothing skills, feelings identification and expression, communication skills, and boundaries. skills can also be useful for many attachment children.

There is a lot of information and many resources available for therapists on teaching these skills. Many child therapists will have their own favorites. I therefore will only briefly describe below some of the strategies I use regularly in these areas. Therapists are encouraged to find their own go-to strategies.

Self-Regulation/Self-Soothing

Self-Regulation/Self-Soothing skills are taught and practiced throughout the course of therapy.

- Breathing is key to self-regulation - It is important to teach breathing skills. Some possible ways of teaching these skills are:
  - Teaching through psychoeducation, demonstration and instruction of belly breathing or diaphragmatic breathing.
  - Breathing together: practice breathing with therapist, parent and child holding hands. The parent and child follow the therapist as the therapist raises arms up, and breathes in, and lowers the arms down and breathes out. The raising and lowering of the arms helps encourage diaphragmatic breathing. This exercise also allows the therapist to easily pace the breathing, while the hand holding and synchronizing of the breath with parent and child are nice attachment pieces.
  - Flower and candle: Have the child and parent practice breathing in through their noses, as if they are smelling a flower, and breath out through their mouths, as if they are blowing out candles.

- Breath counting: Count child and parent through breathing, "In two three four, hold two three four, out two three four."
• Progressive relaxation - Attachment injured children are often too anxious to participate well in guided imagery relaxation, but progressive relaxation with the focus on tightening and relaxing various muscles moving up and down the body can be effective.
• Physical exercise - Physical exercise can help the child regulate in the moment and over the long term. Work with parent and child in identifying physical activity that the child can engage in regularly, as well as specific things they can do when the child finds him or herself get frustrated or tense, such as jumping jacks or running around the yard. Practice in session when appropriate.
• Other self-soothing strategies may include counting, identifying/implementing soothing activities, sensory activities, physical activities, and self-talk.

Therapists can find many resources for learning and teaching breathing and other self-calming skills online. Therapists should find several strategies that they are comfortable with, and practice regularly in session with parent and child. Repetition is important in teaching the skills and increasing the chance the child will be able to recall and implement the skills when stressed. If the child is able to be cooperative with the parent, have them practice at home. The more the child can practice, the better.

Feeling Identification and Expression

Once again there are many resources available for teaching these skills. Some useful interventions include:

- Feelings Charades - Have a list of eight to ten feelings for all to see for reference, and cards with those same feelings on them. Have each person in turn pick a feeling card, and act out that feeling while the others try to guess the feeling.
- Feelings Matching Game - Have pairs of feeling cards. Mix them up and place them face down. Like any memory game, take turns picking pairs and trying to find a match. If someone gets a match, they say a time when they felt that way, and they keep those cards. They can choose not to say a time they felt that way, but then they have to put the cards they picked back where they got them. Contrary to other memory games, if the person gets a match, they do not go again, the play passes on to the next person, so that more people get turns. Sometimes a child may purposely not pick matches to avoid sharing feelings. In this case, use the Feeling Cards game, described below, the next time.
- Feeling Cards - Have a set of feeling cards. Spread the cards with just the backs showing and have the parent pick a card. The parent then tells the child a time they felt that way, starting with, "I felt happy when..." Then the child tells the parent a time they felt that way. Next turn, the child picks the card, but, again, both parent and child tell about a time they felt that way. The play goes back and forth until all the cards are gone. The therapist can also participate if it would be helpful to model this for the child and/or parent. This activity can be extended to include reflective listening skills described below in communication skills.
- Feeling Cards In-the-Moment - Use the feeling cards during the session. Once the child is familiar with the cards, they can be used in the moment to help the child express themselves. For instance, if the child experienced a difficult event during the week, it may be helpful to pull

out the feeling cards and go through them one by one, asking, "Did you feel (emotion) when that happened?", and separating out the cards that they acknowledge. At the end, the therapist can reflect back the feelings, "Oh, so you felt sad and mad and scared when..." The therapist can further help the child explore their feelings by asking further questions like, "What was scary about that for you?" or "What was the saddest part for you?" It can also be a good opportunity to talk about mixed feelings and how one often has several different, and possibly conflicting, feelings at the same time.

Communication Skills

The therapist can keep this very simple with the below exercise, and in-the-moment coaching.

- Reflective Listening Skills - Have the child tell the parent a time they had fun, starting with, "I had fun when..." Have the parent reflect back what they heard, starting with "I heard you say that you had fun when..." Let the child confirm or clarify. Then have a parent say a time they had fun and coach the child to reflect back in the same way. Early in the therapy, start with easy/comfortable feelings like fun, happy, excited. When the child and parent seem ready, the therapist can include more challenging feelings like sad, mad and disappointed. The therapist can have the parent and child pick from feeling cards to help determine which feeling to use. Always be sure the child and parent reflect the feeling they heard when reflecting back to the other.
- In-the-Moment Coaching - The reflective listening skills exercise gets the child and parent ready for in-the-moment coaching during other discussions, to reflect back what the other said. For instance, a child might

express anger about something that happened in the home. The therapist can then coach the parent to reflect back what they heard the child say before responding themselves, and vice versa. This can be very useful in facilitating understanding between parent and child, and can sometimes slow down an otherwise volatile conversation.

Boundaries

Attachment injured children often have unclear boundaries with peers and/or adults. There are many activities and guidelines for teaching boundaries to children. Two useful ones are listed below.

- Boundaries Circles Psychoeducation - Explain circles of familiarity wherein a diagram with concentric circles is labeled from most intimate (family) in the center to least intimate (strangers) on the outside. Facilitate discussion regarding appropriate behavior with those in each of the circles, including appropriate touch.
- Boundary Walk - In this exercise explain how different people have different comfort levels with physical closeness, and their comfort level is also determined by where people fall in the boundary circles (see above). In this exercise, have two people face each other about 5 feet apart. One of the people is the controller and instructs the other person to take a small step forward, then evaluates their comfort level. If comfortable, they then direct the other person to take another step forward. This continues until the controller has decided that they have reached the limit of their comfort level. The two people then repeat the exercise with the other person as the controller. They can then see how their comfort levels are the same or different.

In a session with the therapist, parent and child, start with the parent and therapist in order to demonstrate and role model for the child, then the parent and child, and finally the therapist and child.

This can also be done with the individuals side to side rather than facing each other, and it can be noted how the comfort level can be different side to side rather than face to face. Discussion can then ensue regarding the differences in comfort level and how to respect other people's boundaries and have other people respect our boundaries.

- Discussion and Skill Building Regarding Touch -Include good touch/bad touch, how to stay safe and set boundaries with others, and how to get help if needed.

Social Skills

Depending on the child's functioning and needs, social skills can be useful. The therapist may choose to focus on peer social skills if social stressors are causing distress or concerns in the child's life. As the child becomes more securely attached to their primary care giver, the child will likely become more competent in peer relations and more resilient in the face of peer challenges. Like other areas of skill building there are many resources for therapists to draw on. Some useful interventions are as follows:

- Role Play - For social skills, role play real life situations that the child is experiencing. Allow the child to play a peer and the parent or therapist can play the child, modeling different types of behavior and responses, depending on the concern. The parent may need modeling and coaching to be effective here. The child then plays him or herself, practicing the different responses.

- CBT Role Play - For children who are highly reactive to their peers, implement CBT (Cognitive Behavioral Therapy) role play. First, provide psychoeducation on the CBT triangle and how thoughts, feelings and actions are connected. Then, act out the child in the role play, stating out loud different ways of thinking, leading to different behavior. For instance, if it is a peer teasing situation, the therapist might say out loud, "Oh, they hate me! Something is wrong with me! Everyone hates me!" and act out resulting behavior. The therapist then acts out a more adaptive response in the face of teasing saying something like, "Oh, wow, they seem to be having a bad day! I wonder what their problem is?!" The therapist, parent and child then discuss how the two responses feel different and lead to different behavior. The child then will have the chance to act out and verbalize more adaptive thoughts and responses.

Psychoeducation

While psychoeducation is embedded throughout the talk portion of the therapy, there are a few specific items that are useful to discuss when appropriate in the therapy as follows.

Shame vs Healthy Guilt

Attachment injured children are often acting from a place of shame. It is important to distinguish between healthy guilt and shame. Healthy guilt is the idea that I have done something wrong, and I feel bad about it. Shame is the idea that I did something wrong, and, therefore, I am bad.

Healthy guilt allows a person to evaluate the situation, make amends if needed, and do something different the next time. Shame gives the person no place to go. If the child did something bad because they are bad, then there is nothing further for them to do. Being bad gives the child no options, other than to continue to be bad. As discussed previously, often one of the core beliefs of attachment injured children is that they are bad. If they do something wrong, this just confirms their "badness" and children who feel they are bad, act badly.

In session, when discussing behavior, it is important to make the distinction between shame and guilt. This can be plainly and simply explained to both parent and child, as the therapist continues to separate the child from their behavior.

Parent/Child Roles

The other area that is ripe for discussion is parent versus child roles. For severely neglected children, there was no distinction in roles. They often had to fend for themselves, and sometimes siblings. They may have had to take care of getting food, finding a place to sleep and getting their basic needs met. This, as one might imagine, produces a lot of anxiety in a child.

The situation now may be very different. The child may be in a different home, or their parents may have been able to step up into the parenting role. The child, however, is still acting from survival instincts, trying to take care of everything and make sure that everything is OK. They may have no idea of appropriate child/parent roles.

This can be addressed throughout the therapy by exploring what is different now. That is, exploring how the parenting situation is different, and how the parent is capable of taking charge and taking care of things. The parent can be encouraged to reassure the child that they are capable of handling whatever needs arise.

It also can be addressed through direct psychoeducation on the role of parent and child. Clarify through discussion with parent and child what are the parent's roles and responsibilities and what are the child's roles and responsibilities. The therapist might discuss briefly what roles are, and ask parent and child what they feel their own roles and responsibilities are as parent and child. The therapist can ask questions to the parent and child such as:

> Is it Mom's job or Jessica's job to make sure there is food in the house?
> That's right! And Mom, is that something you can do?
> And as a kid, what is Jessica's job?" (answers may be to go to school, grow, learn, play, do chores...)

Brainstorming and making lists of the roles of family members may be useful. The child can be reassured that they no longer need to worry about a lot of things and that the parent(s) will make sure these things are taken care of.

It can also be useful to use the metaphor of a sports team wherein everyone works together, but the parents are the coaches; the parents are ultimately in charge and always have final say.

Opportunities to explore parent/child roles and the question of who is in charge in the family may come up repeatedly in the therapy. Remember that repetition is good and it will take time for the child to understand and adjust to their role and fully trust that their parents will really take care of things.

Clarifying Responsibility

The question of responsibility is addressed throughout the discussions of the child's history. It is always emphasized that children are never responsible for the behavior of adults. Responsibility, however, may be a difficult concept for the child to fully grasp. They may take responsibility for things that they are not responsible for, such as a peer calling them a name, while, at the same time, not take responsibility for their own behavior. It can be useful, therefore, to address the concept of responsibility independent of the child's history through the Who's Responsible intervention.

• Who's Responsible - In this psychoeducation exercise, the therapist has a list of situations prepared. The situations should not use the names of people actually in the child's life. The therapist may write these out on cards and have the parent and child choose cards to discuss, or the therapist may simply present the situations to the parent and child for discussion. Discussion then ensues on who is responsible for what. For example, one situation may be as follows:

Jessie called Hannah stupid, and Hannah hit Jessie. Who is responsible for what?

This may seem like an easy question to answer, but the child may feel that Jessie is responsible for Hannah hitting him, or that Hannah may have done something that made her responsible for Jessie calling her stupid. In the discussion, it can be clarified that Jessie is responsible for calling Hannah stupid, while Hannah is responsible for hitting Jessie. It can be discussed that only Hannah can be responsible for hitting Jessie, because only Hannah is inside of Hannah's body. Only Hannah can control what her hands do. Only Jessie can be responsible for calling Hannah stupid, because only Jessie is responsible for what comes out of his mouth.

The therapist can then move on to the next situation, or can allow the discussion to expand into discussions about feelings vs actions (i.e. Hannah may have felt like hitting Jessie, but that is not the same as hitting Jessie); impulse control; and problem solving. What could Hannah have done instead? What could Jessie have done instead?

The types and complexity of the situations presented can be tailored to the needs of the particular child.

Addressing Behavior

Much of the child's behavior (home, school, community) is addressed through separate work with the parents when possible (Please see Chapter 8: Working with Parents and Other Caregivers). While it can be important to address behavior in the child/parent session as well, it is important that the child/parent sessions NOT become about the child's misbehavior. Too much focus on behavioral problems with the child can actually increase the behavior. With very young children, perhaps 4- and 5-year-olds, it may not be necessary to discuss the child's behavior in the parent/child session at all. In this case, the parent/child session is focused on attachment and skill building while support around behavior is provided in the parent only sessions.

For most children, however, it is important at times to discuss their behavior in session, otherwise it can become the elephant in the room, particularly if more extreme behaviors are occurring. It can also be useful for setting goals in the therapy and monitoring progress. It is important that there be an expectation set in the therapy of no secrets. Part of the goal in discussing behavior is to help the child be able to tolerate those discussions. Thus, it is particularly important for the therapist to take a stance of acceptance and curiosity. Shaming and blaming are avoided, and understanding the behavior, what drives the behavior, and how to address the underlying issues or emotions, become the goals.

The therapist wants to unravel the behavior sequence to its source and the likely maladaptive thoughts or beliefs that support it. It is important to hold off addressing outside (home, community, school) behavior in the session until after the story of love and attachment narrative have been explored and the child is reasonably cooperative with the attachment-based play and feeding and attachment questions (the frame) and skill building activities.

During the initial period of therapy, the parent sessions can be very important in providing support to the parent regarding the child's behavior, particularly if the child is displaying extreme behaviors. In the parent/child sessions, some ways behavior can be addressed are through discussion, problem solving, externalizing anger, success focused questions and 'no set to yes set' interventions.

Discussing Behavior in the Parent/Child Session

Whenever discussing behavior in an M-MAT parent/child session, the therapist wants to achieve the following:

- Clarify causality through questions - Attachment injured children often have difficulty connecting their behavior to the consequences of their behavior, thus impairing their ability to learn from their experience.
- Explore how behavior causes problems for the child - Often parents and others try to tell the child how their behavior has caused problems for others (parents, family, peers), but early in the therapy the child may not care, and may even be pleased to be causing others distress

due to their anger and defense against their own pain, and/or a sense of power from their effect upon others. So, initially focus on how the behavior is causing problems for the child, and try to move the child to a place of enlightened self-interest.

- Explore what need the child is trying to meet.
- Clarify and explore how parent and child want the same thing - In reality, any reasonably healthy parent wants their child to be happy and well and to be able to participate and be a part of the family. They want them to be able to have good relationships and have good experiences. Children, ultimately, want the same thing.
- Clarifying parental intention, i.e., that the parents are trying to help the child - The child's perception is often that the parent wants them to be miserable, particularly when imposing any kind of consequence. The parent's intentions in imposing consequences, however, is ultimately to help the child learn and to be healthier and happier.

It is also important to provide positive praise for the child's attempts and improvement in engaging in the discussion. The therapist shapes the child's behavior towards constructive conversation using verbal praise or acknowledgement. The therapist also uses questions to help the child make the cause and effect connection between the child's behavior and consequences, natural or otherwise. This is to help the child move from a victim position to an empowered position where they actually do have some control in their lives. Finally the therapist externalizes the behavior, emphasizing that the behavior is the problem, not the child.

As an example, a child may come in upset that they were unable to participate in a family outing. Underlying this upset is the idea that the parent does not like them and wants to exclude them. Now, before addressing this, the therapist, parent and child engage in the attachment-based play. If far enough along in the therapy, the child will be used to this and will likely engage. As always, though, they can choose not to, and the therapist and parent will engage.

The talk part of the session then may go something like this:

Mom: Brian is mad because he didn't get to go to ice cream with us last night.
Therapist: Oh, Brian is mad about missing ice cream. How come Brian missed ice cream last night?
Mom: Well, we were all getting ready to go, then Brian decided he didn't want to put his shoes on and threw a fit!
Brian: NOT AH! YOU WOULDN'T LET ME PUT MY SHOES ON!
Mom: Brian, that is not true, I even brought them down for you!
Therapist: Oh, so Mom, you wanted Brian to go and even brought him his shoes!
Brian: Brooding silence.

Attachment injured children often have a deficit in cause and effect reasoning. With any maladaptive behavior the therapist clarifies in the session, through questions, the cause and effect of consequences related to the behavior. The therapist initially emphasizes how the behavior is causing problems for the child as opposed to how it is causing problems for the family and/or parent. If the child is angry, or needing a sense of power and control, the child may be pleased on some level that the behavior is causing disruption to family or parent. Therefore, the therapist moves the conversation to how it is causing the child a problem as so:

Mom: Brian threw a fit, wouldn't put on his shoes, and made us all have to wait for him! (Parent describes how a behavior was disruptive to the family.)

Therapist: OK, so I understand how that fit caused some problem for the family, but how did it cause a problem for Brian?

Then continue the conversation elaborating and clarifying the consequences of the behavior for the child, being careful to separate the child from the behavior and externalize the behavior:

Mom: Well, Brian had to stay home with Nana and couldn't come to ice cream with us.

Therapist: So Mom, are you telling me that if Brian had put his shoes on, not thrown a fit, he could have gone to ice cream with you?

Mom: Of Course!

Therapist: And Brian, are you saying you wanted to go to ice cream?

Brian: Silence

Therapist: So what I am hearing, Brian, is that you could have gone to ice cream if you had put your shoes on. I wonder why you chose to not put them on? (Emphasizing the child's choice here, and thus his power.)

Brian: Silence

Therapist: So Mom, would you have liked Brian to be able to go with you?

Mom: Well yes, but not if he is going to throw a fit!

Therapist: OK, but in the best possible world, you would really like it if you could take your little boy to ice cream?

Mom: Yes, I would love to be able to have Brian join us!

Therapist: And if he hadn't thrown a fit about his shoes he could have gone?

Mom: Yes, of course!

Therapist: Then you could have had fun together! (emphasize fun)

Mom: Yes.

Therapist: OK, so what I am hearing is that you would love to have Brian go to ice cream with you, and Brian would like to go to ice cream too, so you both want the same thing! Isn't that great that you both want the same thing! Now we just need to figure out what is getting in the way...Hmmm...It seems like that fit got in the way! That fit sure kept you from getting what you both wanted!

So here the therapist has clarified the cause and effect (fit resulted in child not going to ice cream), emphasized that the parent and child want the same thing, and also externalized the behavior (it was the fit that was the problem, not Brian). The therapist can then explore what needs the child was trying to meet through the fit.

Therapist: Hmmm, I'm really curious why Brian didn't want to put his shoes on...Brian, how come you didn't want to put your shoes on?

The therapist gives the child a chance to respond. If the child does not respond, or if the response seems ingenuine:

Therapist: Mom, do you have an idea as to why Brian didn't want to put his shoes on? (Parents often have good insight into their child's behavior.)

Mom: I think he was mad at me because he didn't want to stop playing and put away his toys.

Therapist: Oh, so maybe anger got in the way (externalizing anger). It can be hard to have to stop playing and put away toys when you're in the middle of something (empathy). That can be really frustrating.

Brian: I was making a star station!

Mom: Brian was building with his blocks and there were pieces everywhere. I asked him to pick them up before we left.

We are now ready to begin problem solving.

Problem Solving

Problem solving techniques are the same in M-MAT as in any other therapy. The therapist helps the child and family generate possible solutions, evaluate the options and role play solutions. In role playing it is usually helpful to the child for the therapist or parent to role-play and model the solution before asking the child to do so.

Remember that repetition, as always, is important. The therapist can set up homework that parent and child practice certain solutions or skills outside of the session as well. While a child may be able to practice skills and solutions when calm and in session, when the child is angry, it is another matter. It is therefore helpful to address anger separately, head on.

Externalizing Anger

The child's anger may sabotage the child's ability to moderate their behavior. I have had many children tell me that they feel they have more anger inside than anyone else in the world. While M-MAT itself should help reduce this anger, it can also be helpful to specifically externalize and address the child's anger directly.

First, it is important to understand the purpose and power of anger. The child's anger has become a defender, protector, and even a friend. It gives the child a sense of power when they would otherwise feel powerless, helpless and vulnerable. It tries desperately to protect the child's sense of self. It can become addictive with its resulting adrenaline and sense of power. To act out in an angry way, to throw things and knock things over and scream and yell, in the moment, feels good. More adults would probably do so if there were not so many consequences associated with it!

The child's anger is often displaced anger. It can feel right in the moment because it is related to an earlier situation where anger was an appropriate response. For instance, a child that was verbally abused when young may be over reactive and angry in certain situations because it reminds them of the early situation and, psychologically, they are back there in that situation.

The problem with anger is that it is a trickster. Like many addictions, it can bring relief in the moment, but in the long run can cause more distress, lower self-worth, and greater life disruption.

- Externalizing Anger Role Play - One intervention that has been effective in helping children with their anger is the Externalizing Anger Role Play. It involves externalizing anger and giving the anger and the child a voice through role play using small figures, such as sand tray figures. The process is as follows:

   Identify a situation that has brought up a lot of anger for the child (this may often come up spontaneously in the session as behavior is discussed). Discuss briefly how anger can cause problems for people and sometimes anger is a trickster. That is, sometimes it tells us to do things that aren't good for us. Sometimes it lies to us. Ask the child to pick a figure for him or herself, with the direction that it has to be a positive figure. Ask the child to also pick a figure for anger. Have the child pick any other figure(s) necessary for the role play.

As an example, perhaps the child gets very angry when the child hears 'no' from a parent. The therapist can have the parent take the parent figure the child has picked out, have the child take the figure for themselves, and the therapist can take the figure for anger.

Have the parent and child start to act out the role play with the figures:

Parent and child figures are facing each other.

Parent: "No, you can't go to Suzie's house, it is almost dinner time."

The therapist jumps in with the "Anger" figure, talking to the child figure, saying some possible cognitive distortions that anger could be saying: "That's not fair! Mom can't tell you what to do! She hates you! She never lets you do anything! Scream and yell because it's not fair!"

This externalizing of the anger and verbalizing cognitive distortions usually gives the child pause. The therapist can stop and ask the child, "Hmmm...Do you think what anger is saying is true?"

Anger can then jump back in and say to the child figure, "Don't listen to her! She's not your friend! I'm your only friend! You're powerful and strong with me!"

Therapist: "Hmmm, it sounds like anger is trying to trick you. What do you think is really true?"

Discussion and role play can continue as appropriate. At some point the therapist can ask the child to use the child figure to talk back to anger. To take a stand. To tell anger what is really true. To stand up to anger. The therapist can model this as well.

Through this type of role play, using figures, the child, therapist and parent align in confronting the cognitive distortions that feed the anger.

It is important to use the figures for this intervention as the therapist would not want to state the cognitive distortions directly to the child as there is not enough separation and it could be counterproductive. By using the figures, everything is externalized from the child and can be observed and processed through this type of play. Imaginative play is one of the ways children naturally process their experiences.

The child's anger has likely been with the child for a long time, and is not going to give up without a fight. This exercise, however, gives parent, child and therapist a common language in discussing anger. The therapist can in subsequent sessions reference how anger seems to be causing problems again or inquire about time during the week when the child was able to stand up to anger; when they could have acted out through anger but chose something different. The parent also can reference standing up to anger when they see their child starting to get angry outside of the session, or notice them managing their anger well.

Success Focused Questions

One way to avoid focusing too much on negative behavior is by focusing on the successes or exceptions to the behavior challenges. Depending on the specific challenges, the therapist may check in with the parent and child regularly on times the child was successful in addressing or reducing specific behaviors that had been identified. Below are some sample questions for both the parent and child:

> Can you think of a time that you handled anger well this week?
> Can you think of a time that your child could have lied, but chose to tell the truth?

Tell me about a time this week that Ellie got along with her sister.

What is a time you cooperated this week?

Follow up questions may explore the why, when and how of the child's success.

The reality is that no matter how problematic a child's behavior is, there are always times when their behavior is appropriate. Exploring these times can strengthen progress, and supports a new story for the child.

Give Backs

Sometimes the child has acted out in a way that is hurtful to the family, parent, or family member. Examples may be destroying property (i.e., intentionally breaking something that belongs to a parent or sibling), creating a disruption where the whole family has to change plans (i.e., acting out at an event wherein the whole family has to leave with the child) or physical aggression.

In these circumstances the M-MAT therapist talks about "givebacks" which is a common strategy used in attachment-based parenting. Givebacks are therapeutically important for the child. The child will likely feel shame regarding the behavior, even if they appear shameless. Their own behavior has confirmed to them that they are bad, an underlying core belief. Givebacks allow the child to atone for their behavior and to be forgiven and forgive themselves so that they can move on and not continue to escalate.

In the therapy session, explain that when one person hurts or takes away from another, they have to give back to that person. The child, with the help of the parent, can brainstorm ideas for give backs (i.e., doing sister's chores, sweeping the deck for Mom, repairing damages with dad).

It is explained, however, that it is not up to the child to decide what the giveback should be. The child can give suggestions, but it is the parent possibly with the injured party (i.e., a sibling) who gets to make the final decision on what the giveback should be, because they are the injured party.

Ideally the therapist will have previously explained the concept of givebacks to the parent in the parent session, emphasizing the fact that following through with their child on completing the giveback often entails more work for the parent. Follow through is important, however, as the giveback is a therapeutic intervention for the child.

No Set to Yes Set

Sometimes children are automatically oppositional. That is, they say no to just about anything their parents say. It has become habitual. Their neural pathways for a "no" response are well entrenched, while "yes" responses are rather foreign to their brain. For younger children in particular, it can be helpful to play a game to try it increase yes responses. In this game the therapist introduces it as a game with a great deal of excitement:

Therapist: (to child) We're going to play a game! In this game I'm going to ask you to do something, and you are going to say, "OK!" and then see how fast you can do it. So, James, can you get me that ball over there? (all spoken with enthusiasm).
Child starts to get the ball.
Therapist: Remember, say, "OK" (upbeat tone).
James: OK!
Therapist: Great! Now bring me the ball!
Child complies.
Therapist: Oh, good job!

Therapist: Mom, can you ask James to do something?
Mom: James, clap your hands 2 times! (with continued enthusiasm).
Child starts to comply
Therapist: Say "OK"
James: "OK"
Child complies.
Therapist and Mom: Yay! Fantastic!

Continue to alternate between the parent and the therapist giving directions to the child.

Parents are often shocked that this works and their child is complying with requests. This intervention has been used with children up to age 7, and, to date, it has always been successful. While this, by itself, will not necessarily translate to more cooperation at home, it can be played periodically throughout the therapy and can be helpful for the habitually oppositional child.

Another game that is good for addressing oppositional behavior is the adaptation of "Mother May I" which can be found in Appendix A: Attachment-Based Play Activities.

Conclusion

In summary, attachment talk is the middle part of an M-MAT session. It includes re-storying, skill building, psychoeducation, and addressing behavior. The story of love and the attachment narrative are always the first interventions of the talk therapy that the therapist implements with parent and child. The talk portion of the therapy is always framed by the attachment-based play at the beginning, and the feeding and attachment questions at the end.

8

Working with Parents

Parents, or other primary caregivers, are instrumental in their child's therapy and healing. Parents do not need to be perfect to be effective. They do not even need to be exceptional. They do need to have the capacity to form an attachment with their child, and be reasonably psychologically healthy in order to be an instrument in their child's healing. Most parents can meet these criteria.

The M-MAT therapist has three major tasks in their individual work with parents. The first task is to get the parents on board with Multi-Modal Attachment Therapy (M-MAT); the second is to convey some attachment-based parenting principals; and the third is to provide parent support.

Getting the Parents on Board

The first step in getting parents on board is understanding the parent's perspective. Often, the parents of attachment injured children feel like failures. They have likely taken a child into their home to offer them a good life and a good future. They have used their parenting skills, which may have been quite effective with other children, only to find the attachment injured child is disconnected, aggressive or passive aggressive, angry, hurt and hurting. They may even know something about attachment and have attempted to connect with their child in an attachment oriented way, only to be rejected.

For biological parents who have changed their lives and are now ready to parent their child, guilt is often a strong force to be contended with. Guilt and shame can sabotage their parenting efforts. They may be too lenient in their parenting out of a sense of guilt. They may feel incapable out of a sense of shame. It is important to help these parents use their sense of guilt to help them to make changes in their parenting that are most beneficial to their child, and to let go of shame altogether.

The attachment injured child can be a master at pulling their parents into power struggles. Parents may be unable to manage extreme behaviors and feel very out of control. The child may be disruptive to the whole family. It is not unusual to find the whole family revolving around responding to, or trying to manage, the child's behavior.

To make matters worse, everyone has an opinion on how to better parent their child. The child may be quite well behaved and even charming with others, but act out in the extreme with the primary caregiver. This leads others to believe that the parent must be doing something wrong. Parents often feel isolated and blamed.

In order to gain some kind of control and order, some parents may go to more extreme parenting strategies or use harsher consequences than they would otherwise, or than they feel good about. Of course this only makes things worse, playing into the child's mindset that they are bad, and their parents are bad.

Many parents feel hopeless. Everything they have tried has failed, including other therapies. They may be trying this therapy as a last ditch effort to save their child and their family. It is useful to give them hope; to let them know that M-MAT has helped others in their situation. It is common for parents to come to the first session expressing their commitment to their child. By about the fourth or fifth session, once they are more comfortable and familiar with the therapist, and before seeing any significant change in their child, they may express that they are not sure that they can do it. They are not sure if they can parent this child. They are losing hope. Often shortly after this, the child makes their first significant shift.

A useful strategy is to ask parents to give M-MAT 10 weeks total before they make any decision regarding their child. By then there should be some indication that the therapy is working. In the larger scheme of the child's and family's life, 10 weeks is not very long. It can also be helpful to discuss the process of change, and that it is not likely to be linear. The child is likely to make progress gradually, and will have setbacks and bad days along the way.

It is important for the therapist to listen, really listen, without judgement, to what the parents have to say. The assessment is a good time to form a therapeutic alliance with the parents, as the therapist gathers information to determine the needs of the child and family. Acceptance and empathy during this process are crucial.

Once the therapist has determined, through a thorough assessment, that they are looking at a child with attachment injuries, it is time to provide psychoeducation to the parent. The therapist empathizes with the parents' struggles using deep empathy skills. The therapist can then help the parents understand attachment and the child's perspective through psychoeducation.

Information from this book and from any other reputable sources on attachment can be used to educate parents. The therapist can let parents know that their child needs more than traditional therapy, and until the child's attachment injuries are healed, standard parenting practices are likely to be ineffective, though there are things they can do to help their child. Often the parents will feel some relief in gaining a better understanding of their child.

Something that is both important and exciting to let the parents know is that they are instrumental in the healing of their child and essential to their child's therapy. Because their child was injured through relationship, much of their healing must come through relationship.

The final step in getting parents on board with M-MAT is explaining the therapy to them. Explain the process and the frame. Explain the rationale. Explain that the attachment play and feeding are regressive, and that the attachment narrative will address difficult topics. Explain that the child can choose or not choose to participate and that M-MAT uses fun and enthusiasm to engage the child. Ask the parent to allow the therapist to direct the session. Let the parent know that, for the time of the parent/child session, they can be out of the disciplinarian role so that they can focus on the attachment between parent and child. Let parents know that the therapist will address any child behaviors in the session that need addressing (many parents are quite happy to be relieved of discipline duties for that period!).

Below is a summary of the steps in getting the parent on board:

1. Understand the parent's perspective.
2. Communicate acceptance and empathy for parent.

3. Provide psychoeducation regarding attachment and the child's perspective.
4. Let parents know that they are instrumental in their child's healing.
5. Explain M-MAT.

Attachment-Based Parenting

Any successful parenting is based on a good relationship between parent and child. Often, once attachment issues are resolving, as long as the parents practice good parenting skills, they will be able to be effective. Not all parents have good parenting skills, however, and attachment-based practices are useful in parenting children with attachment injuries. There are a lot of resources available on parenting and attachment-based parenting. Please access other resources as needed.

Following are a few practices, both general parenting practices and attachment-based practices, that I have gathered along the way and discuss regularly with parents.

Monitor for Safety

Any child who has experienced early trauma is likely to be very sensitive to the possibility of threat. Monitor for conditions that may lead to the child feeling unsafe, either physically or emotionally. This may include apparently innocuous factors such as voice tone or facial expression of the parent. Other factors may include yelling, chaotic or unexpected changes, exposure to television or media violence or sexual content, aggressive siblings or peers, and any number of other factors. Your child may have some triggers that are very specific to them. Work to create a safe, calm environment for your child. Provide comfort and reassurance when needed. Note that children with attachment injuries may reject a parent's attempts to comfort, but make the attempt anyway, always being respectful of the child's boundaries.

Build Touch Into Your Day

Rub your child's back at bedtime. Give your child a hug in the morning or after school. Come up with a special handshake. Use high-fives indiscriminately. Rock your child if appropriate. Put your hand on your child's shoulder. Do what you can to provide safe, positive touch every day. This may sound overly simplistic, but it is very, very helpful in developing the attachment between a parent and an attachment injured child.

Proximity: Keep Your Child Near

If your child has difficulty with free time after school, set them up with activities at a table in the same room with you. If your child has difficulty at community events, have your child sit next to you at the event, and hold their hand if appropriate. Require your child to hold on to the cart in the grocery store. If they are playing in another room, go into the other room periodically to check in on them. Any time you are giving your child direction or have something to say to them, make sure you are near your child and making eye contact. Move down to your child's level when possible. Do not shout directions across the room.

Always Show Up

This is important for all children, but especially attachment injured children. Attachment injured children have often been disappointed by parents/caregivers many times in their lives. They may not expect you to follow through. If you say you are going to be there, be there. If you are going to be away from your child for a period, let them know how frequently and approximately when you will call them (i.e., every evening...), then call. Even if the child does not have anything to say on the phone, even if they seem unhappy to disrupt what they were doing to talk to you, even if they do not seem happy to hear from you, call anyway and let them know that you are thinking about them and love them.

Life does happen, and sometimes a parent cannot follow through due to emergency circumstances. In these instances, communicate with the child as soon as reasonably able. Apologize. Let them know that you wanted to be with them and if you could have you would have. If appropriate, reschedule.

Reconnect After an Absence

You come home after an absence and you find your child turns away from you and avoids eye contact. It might be tempting to move on to something else. Don't. Engage them playfully, tickle them gently or say playfully, "I'm gonna get you!" and embrace them in a big bear hug. It's up to the parent to re-connect. For regular absences, such as school, set up some kind of a re-engagement ritual. It could be as simple as a high five or hand shake, or hug or a "tell me about your day" routine.

Deep Empathy

You may have a hard time understanding where your child is coming from. Perhaps you had very different childhood experiences, or you feel you would never have behaved like your child behaves. Empathy can be defined as understanding how you would feel in your child's situation.

Deep empathy can be further defined as understanding how your child feels in that situation.

Deep Empathy requires that you take yourself out of your own experience and into your child's. Perhaps under your child's anger is fear or anxiety. When your child says, "You hate me!" and you know this is the farthest thing from the truth, it can be tempting to argue with them or negate that idea. Instead, you can validate the child's feeling or experience without saying that it is true. This opens up the communication rather than shutting it down.

For instance, when your child says, "You hate me!" you can respond, "Gosh, that would be so hard to feel like I hate you. I'm so sorry you feel that way, I can imagine how hurtful that would feel." Thus, you have acknowledged their experience without saying it is true, and without negating or arguing.

You can then say what is true from your perspective, if it seems useful, using clear "I" statements and owning your own experience, i.e., "For me, when I look at you I feel a lot of love. Sometimes I feel frustration when you aren't following directions, but always I feel love for you."

Consistency

Consistency is important for all children, but especially important for attachment injured children. Say what you mean, mean what you say, and always follow through. Attachment injured children generally have the experience that parents or caregivers are extraordinarily inconsistent. Consistent structure helps them, inconsistent structure will likely make things worse.

Sometimes parents of attachment injured children get so frustrated with their children that they set consequences that they regret (i.e., you are grounded for a month!). In these instances, you can allow your child to earn their way back into good graces. This can be through doing chores, demonstrating cooperation in some specific way, etc. Whatever you choose, it needs to be very clear, and clearly stated to the child, so there are no surprises.

Holiday and Family Functions

Attachment injured children should always be included in family and holiday functions when possible. Loss of these should never be used as a consequence. If your child is having difficulty managing their behavior, then you may need to set some structure around the event. For instance the child may need to stay near you the whole time, and/or the child's time may need to be limited. These accommodations should always be framed as an attempt to help the child have a good time, not as a consequence. The message should be that the child is wanted and that the parent will do what they can to help them be successful. If the child simply is not able to manage, the message should be, "We'll try again next time."

Limit Choices and Things

Attachment injured children are notorious for having meltdowns when they have too many choices. If you can, limit choices to two or three options. This goes for toys too. Having too many toys available just seems to create chaos for the child. If the child has a lot of toys, you may want to rotate them, putting out a smaller selection of toys at a time.

Sometimes parents want to make up for the child's early deprivation by providing an overabundance at birthdays or holidays. This is not a useful strategy for the attachment injured child. An overemphasis on things is counter to developing a healthy relationship between parent and child. The child will usually do best with a small, contained celebration where the emphasis is on celebrating family and child.

Your Attention and Emotional Intensity - Attention as Gold

Unless your attachment injured child is 100% disengaged, the coin of the realm is attention and emotional intensity. Be aware of where your attention goes. If it is constantly focused on negative behavior, then that behavior is likely to increase. Classroom studies bear this out, with behavior difficulties significantly lower in classrooms with a high ratio of positive comments to corrective comments. Some negative behaviors can be strategically ignored, while positive behaviors are given more attention.

That being said, children with attachment injuries often do not do well with overt or excessive praise because it creates cognitive dissonance. That is, it is at odds with their own internal beliefs about themselves. Sometimes an attachment injured child will act out after being given praise. A good way to acknowledge positive behavior without triggering resistance within your child is to just 'notice' it or acknowledge it in an understated way as in the following examples:

> I noticed you played well with your brother today.
> I appreciate your help with the groceries.
> Thanks for being quiet so I could read this.
> Good job following directions.
> Good idea.
> Good thinking.
> Thanks!
> Good for you!

Give Clear, Concise Directions

Before giving a direction, make sure you have your child's attention, use eye contact if possible, keep your directions short. Do not string multiple directions together. Use please and thank you as a matter of course. Give the child time to respond.

Emphasize the Child's Choices

Emphasize choice. We are trying to help the child feel more empowered by understanding that what the child does makes a difference. The child always has choices and each choice has subsequent consequences, i.e., "You can put your shoes on and come to ice cream with us or you can stay home with Nana, your choice". As another example, you may have a rule that if the child does not get ready for school on time, the next day the child will have to get up earlier to get ready for school. If the child is delaying getting ready for school, the parent can say something like, "Oh, it looks like you are choosing to get up earlier tomorrow so you'll have enough time to get ready." Or if the child is complaining about a consequence, the parent can say, "I'm sorry you made that choice," or, "You made that choice when you..."

Use Attachment-Based Rewards

Do not offer things and treats as rewards for good behavior. For attachment injured children it does not work. Do offer extra time together, perhaps doing something special, as a natural positive consequence of the child's cooperation. For instance, "If we get all our chores done by 2pm, you and I can... (make cookies together, play a game together, go out in the back yard together, take a walk or hike together...)" Again, choice can be emphasized when the child earns a positive attachment-based reward, i.e.,"How nice that we can make cookies together! I'm so glad we both chose to get our chores done!"

Stay Out of Power Struggles

Attachment injured children can be masters at engaging parents in power struggles. The following are some strategies to avoid a power struggle:

- Broken Record - Classic strategy in which the parent repeats the direction, calmly, until the child complies. Sometimes it is useful to reflect what the child says, then continue to repeat the direction. An example:

    The parent has already given the child a five minute warning and now it is time for the child to get ready for bed.

    Parent: It's time to get ready for bed.
    Child: That's not fair, I just started this!
    Parent: Nevertheless, it's time to get ready for bed
    Child: Noooooo...I just started!
    Parent: You just started and that is frustrating, but still it is time to get ready for bed.
    Child: YOU'RE MEAN! (Child is looking for a reaction here).
    Parent: I hear you are frustrated, but you still need to get ready for bed.
    Child: I'm not frustrated! You're just mean! (Still trying for the reaction)
    Parent: You need to get ready for bed.

This is a good skill to role play with parents, first letting the parent play the child and the therapist play the parent.

- Disengage, Really Disengage, from the Struggle - Sometimes continued engagement feeds behavior and tantrumming. When a child is in a tantrum they are acting from the more primitive part of their brain and are not able to access their reasoning or self-soothing skills. Sometimes it is important to give them space to calm down. If they have emotionally pushed your buttons, it is even more important to disengage and give yourself time to calm down. Continued engagement in these circumstances often fuels the tantrum.

  If you have discussed "taking a break" ahead of time with your child, this may go more smoothly. In any case, you can state to your child, "I'm going to take a break so we can both calm down. I'll come back and talk with you in a few minutes." During this time, really take a break. If you are still fuming and emotionally engaged even while physically away, the child will pick up on this. If there is something that engages you, like reading a novel, or watching a brief clip on your phone, do this. Use your own self-soothing strategies. And be sure to ALWAYS re-engage. If the child calms down and is playing quietly it can be tempting to just let them be. It is important though for the parent to re-engage the child, otherwise the child learns that they can push away closeness and attachment through tantrums.

  Of course, always be aware of safety. If you are concerned for your child's safety and there is another adult in the house, have them monitor the child without engaging. If that is not possible then stay where you can monitor the child as needed.

- Ignore the Hooks, Cover your Buttons - The child may try to draw you in with barbs or hooks. They may try to push your buttons. Any intense emotional response will feed their sense of power as well as their drive for negative attention. Therefore, it will increase the negative behavior.

• Don't argue - Some children are masters of engaging their parents in arguments. Probably the most effective strategy to circumvent arguments is simply to say, "I'm not going to argue about this," and use the broken record strategy if necessary.

• Let Go of Trying to Control Your Child - One of the things that makes parents most crazy and leads to power struggles is trying to control their child in the moment, which is an impossible feat. You cannot control your child, but you can control the environment of the home and your own responses, which will either increase or decrease behaviors. You can control the structure you set up in your home, your expectations, how you communicate, and how you parent. You can also regain control of the home if the child's behavior has taken control of it. In any given moment, however, you cannot control the child. One of the goals of M-MAT is that your child will gain control of him or herself, with your support.

Limit Media Exposure

The attachment injured child needs safety to heal. This is created by consistency, routine and a stable environment. Violent and sexualized media can sabotage that safety. The attachment injured child may be drawn to violent media. Violent images and media activate stress hormones in the child, never allowing them to truly calm, and triggering anxiety and fear responses.

Work Together

If you have a parenting partner, work together as a team. Do not allow the child to split you. Talk out of ear reach of the child about parenting concerns. Similarly, avoid arguing in front of your child. Back each other up. Provide respite for each other and tag team as needed during difficult behavior.

Take Care of Yourself

Do not be a martyr to your child's behavior. It will only burn you out and make your child worse. Find ways to take care of yourself. While your child is at school, get a massage, go for a walk in nature, have lunch with a friend, read your favorite author. Make a list of activities that are fun and/or nurturing for you. If you have a co-parent, trade off parenting when able or needed. Develop a support network. Find respite opportunities. If you are in a relationship with a spouse or other partner, make time for that relationship. If you have other children, make time for them as well.

These things are often easier said than done, but you can find ways to take care of yourself.

Parent Support

All parents need support, and the saying that it takes a village to raise a child is never more true than with children struggling with attachment injuries. The therapist wants to make sure the parents have adequate support by addressing the following:

Support Network

Help parents to identify and develop their support system, i.e., family, friends, social service and other professionals, teachers and school personnel, other parents, online groups and resources, therapists and other mental health professionals. There are often groups and resources specifically available for adoptive parents and kinship care. Help parents to clarify how to best use the supports available to them.

Respite

Parents often identify respite as one of the most helpful supports for them. If the child is able to manage in various settings, this may mean having the child play at a friend's one day a week (making sure, of course, that this is a reasonably well supervised and safe situation), or attending an after school program several days a week.

Family members or a co-parent may also be willing to spend special time with the child to give the primary caregiver a break.

If the child needs more support, some agencies may have activities that are geared to at-risk children or children with behavioral challenges.

Parents may feel that, due the child's attachment injuries, they need to be with the child all of their available time. This is not true and can be counterproductive. The child needs to know that the parent can be reached and is available if a real need arises, but both parent and child can benefit from some time away.

For successful respite, it is important that the child knows when the parent is leaving and when they will return. It is important that the parent says goodbye before leaving. This may seem self-evident, but sometimes, if the child is in the habit of tantrumming when the parent leaves, and the child is at the moment engaged in some activity, it can be tempting for the parent to just slip out. This should be avoided at all costs. It will too clearly mirror early abandonment scenarios.

If time away is longer than a day, the parent should make arrangements to call in at least once a day to talk to their child. And, as discussed in the previous section on attachment-based parenting, the parent should always re-engage the child upon their reunion, including positive touch when possible.

Therapist Support

The therapist stance with parents should always be one of support. In session, the therapist should endeavor to understand the parents point of view, and use deep empathy skills to express this understanding. The therapist should meet the parent where they are, and, if needed, gently move them towards more effective parenting and useful understanding of their child. As long as they are able to develop an attachment to their child and are reasonably psychologically healthy, the parent or primary caregiver is the best chance the child has for healing and a happy life.

Outside of the session, the extent of therapist support may vary depending on the therapist and client situations. Be sure that parents have any crisis numbers that might be needed at hand, including mental health crisis, and police or sheriff, if indicated. The therapist should be sure to let parents know what their crisis policy is, and who they should contact under what circumstances. Parents should be informed of what the therapist's call back policy is and when the therapist can be reached.

Homework

The only homework that M-MAT requires, aside from parenting suggestions, is for parents to add touch into their relationship with their child, and to provide play and individual time for their child during the week.

What this looks like may vary depending on the child's needs and their reactivity to their parents. Discuss with the parents what might work as far as adding more touch. For one child it may be high fives and a special hand shake. For another child it may be holding and rocking for 10 minutes before bed every night. For yet another child it might just be a gentle hand on the shoulder now and then.

If the child is extremely reactive to the parent, adding one-on-one time may need to wait until the child is more cooperative and less reactive, as demonstrated in the therapy sessions, to increase the likelihood of positive one-on-one time for both parent and child. Of course some children may be ready right away. Once a week of one-on-one time, in addition to the therapy session, is a good goal. As the therapy moves into the last phase and towards closure, this can be increased.

It is also important for there to be some kind of daily check-in between parent and child built into their routine. This could be part of a bedtime routine, or an after school check-in.

Additional homework, if it works for the parent and child, would be to practice skills at home related to skill building activities. This can help the child learn and generalize skills more quickly.

Working with Biological Parents vs Other Caregivers

The dynamic in working with biological parents versus other caregivers can be somewhat different. With biological parents, the therapist is often dealing with the parents' sense of guilt or shame for whatever their child experienced when younger. The biological parent may be someone who is recovering from an addiction, mental illness, or who experienced domestic violence when the child was younger.

All caregivers, not just biological parents, should be screened in the initial assessment for substance use, mental illness and domestic violence concerns. The therapist wants to assure these issues have been, or are being, addressed. This may mean separate individual therapy or treatment for the parent.

Addiction and domestic violence need to be addressed before M-MAT is initiated. A parent or caregiver who is using substances cannot be the present, secure and stable person the child needs. Any violence in the home will also sabotage M-MAT. The attachment injured child needs safety above all else to begin healing.

Biological parents may also be particularly susceptible to guilt and shame regarding their earlier parenting deficits. Help the parents distinguish between guilt and shame (guilt is feeling bad for their mistakes and how they might have hurt their child, shame is the sense that they are bad and bad parents). Help them to let go of the shame, and use the guilt constructively to do something different now.

Guilt can sometimes lead to overly permissive parenting, which is not what any child needs, much less an attachment injured child. The therapist works to help the parent see that what their child needs is firm and consistent parenting.

The attachment injured child may also use the parent's sense of guilt or shame to try and get a reaction from them. Work with the parent specifically on these triggers and how to respond.

Biological parents are also more likely to be triggered in the telling of the child's attachment narrative. Their child's story is also their story. Be sure that the parent understands what the attachment narrative involves. If parents become emotional in the parent/child session, proceed as described in Chapter 7: M-MAT Talk, to help the child understand that the parent is OK, and to have a sense of containment.

With caregivers other than the biological parents, there is a greater chance of the child losing the placement and connection forever, particularly for non-relative placements. If the caregiver sincerely wants to parent the child but is struggling because of the child's behavior, they are a perfect candidate for M-MAT. In these circumstances, offer hope to the caregivers and ask them to engage in M-MAT for at least 10 weeks before making any decision, stating that there should be at least some shift in that period, enough to give hope to the parent/caregiver to continue the therapy.

If the caregiver never really wanted the child, or is not attached or able to attach, then the therapist may quickly find they need to move to M-MAT Individual. Sometimes the parent is upfront with expressions of a lack of attachment, and sometimes not. Sometimes the parent may demonstrate their lack of readiness by simply not showing up and/or missing multiple appointments.

If the parent is sincere in wanting to be able to connect with their child but their own attachment issues are getting in the way, individual therapy for the parent may be indicated. Be careful, however, not to mistake hopelessness, frustration and fatigue as a lack of commitment or attachment on the caregiver's part. If it is a viable home and attachment for the child, all efforts should be made to preserve the placement.

Conclusion

The best chance an attachment injured child has for a happy, healthy life is to develop a positive attachment to their primary caregiver. This forms a solid base for the child's development. Therefore, the parent is crucial in the child's therapy. The M-MAT therapist can help parents help their child by providing psychoeducation regarding attachment theory and the attachment injured child; explaining and encouraging engagement in M-MAT; providing attachment-based parenting education; and working with the parents on parenting support.

9

Putting It All Together

Below are a few notes on putting all of the Multi-Modal Attachment Therapy (M-MAT) pieces together to create a successful therapy for child and parent.

Adjusting for the Child's Age

Five to 12 years is a wide age range in child development terms. When working with children, the therapist should adjust the work according to the child's developmental and emotional age. Generally speaking, with younger children, the session will involve more play and less talk. Older children, 10 through 12 years of age, are more likely to be able to contribute significantly to the attachment narrative than younger children. This is not always the case, however. An extremely bright and insightful 5-year-old may contribute significantly to the talk portion of M-MAT, while a much older child may be initially mute in the sessions. Remember, though, that in the therapy, the parent and therapist are responsible for providing the play opportunities, and re-storying for the child.

Attachment injured children can be pseudo-mature, acting in some ways older than their age and eschewing "baby" things. The therapist should take care not to let this fool them, and make the mistake of shying away from attachment play with these children. When the therapist describes M-MAT to parents, they may state that they do not believe their child will want to participate in the attachment-based play because it is too babyish. To date, I have not found a child who has not ultimately relished this play. Usually the child takes to it right away because it fills such an important, unmet need within them.

Ultimately, use common sense. There may be more holding and rocking with younger children than older. Gauge the child's response. Remember that M-MAT attachment play is by its nature regressive because M-MAT is attempting to heal the younger injured child within any child, so do not be afraid to go young in the play. Complexity of the games can be tailored to the child's developmental level. For instance, for a developmentally young child the therapist may play a patty-cake clapping game with parent and child. For an older child, the therapist may choose to play any of the many more complicated clapping games.

Therapy Timeline

The therapy timeline will vary from child to child, but a sample timeline for parent/child sessions may look like this:

Session 1:

- Attachment-Based Play
- Story of Love
- Feeding and Questions

Sessions 2-4

- Attachment-Based Play
- Attachment Narrative
- Feeding and Questions

Session 5

- Attachment-Based Play
- Self-Soothing Skills
- Feeding and Questions

Session 6

- Attachment-Based Play
- Communication Skills
- Feeding and Questions

Session 7

- Attachment-Based Play
- What Babies Need
- Feeding and Questions

Session 8

- Attachment-Based Play

- Feeling Identification Skills, Self-Soothing Skills (remember, repetition is good).
- Feeding and Questions

Session 9

- Attachment-Based Play
- Addressing Behavior, Self-Soothing Skills
- Feeding and Questions

Session 10

- Attachment Based Play
- Parent/Child Roles
- Feeding and Questions

Session 11...

- Attachment-Based Play
- (Skill Building, Addressing Behaviors, Re-storying, and Psychoeducation, repeating as needed)
- Feeding and Questions

Note that in all sessions, the frame of attachment-based play and feeding and questions is utilized. Once the Story of Love and Attachment Narrative have been completed, the talk portion of the session can move to skill building, psychoeducation and addressing behavior, as needed. Exactly which activity should be planned for each session should be determined by the most pressing needs presented by the child. In general, self-soothing skills should be worked on early in the therapy.

There may be times when returning to the attachment narrative is necessary to fill in missing pieces, or to reference when exploring and striving to understand current behavior, or when pieces of the child's history come up for the child.

Each session should be planned before the session. This will help keep the therapy on track. Of course the therapist may sometimes need to adjust a session at the time, based on immediate needs. The therapist needs to be careful, however, to not end up responding each week to a new 'Crisis of the Week' which can sabotage moving forward in the therapy. In any case, the frame (attachment-based play, and feeding and questions) should always be maintained if at all possible. If the child refuses to cooperate, that is OK, the therapist can engage in these with the parents. The therapist can adjust the play and talk sections, shortening or lengthening each as needed, to address immediate concerns. The frame, however, should still be maintained.

After each session the therapist can reflect on the session in planning the next session.

Summary of M-MAT Talk Topics and Interventions

Below are summaries of topics and interventions for the four areas of M-MAT Talk (Re-Storying, Skill Building, Psychoeducation, and Addressing Behavior) for ease of planning sessions.

Summary of Re-Storying interventions:

- Story of Love
- Attachment Narrative
- What Do Babies Need?
- Heart of Hearts

Summary of Skill Building and Psychoeducation topics:

• Self-Regulation/Self-Soothing
• Feeling Identification and Expression
• Communication Skills
• Boundaries
• Social Skills
• Shame vs Healthy Guilt
• Parent/Child Roles
• Clarifying Responsibility

Summary of Addressing Behavior interventions:

• Discussion
• Problem Solving
• Externalizing Anger
• Success Focused Questions
• Give Backs
• No Set to Yes Set

Sample Session Plan

Always have the session planned ahead of time. Both the play and talk sections should be planned. The therapist should also have the snack planned, and, if they are new to M-MAT, it can be helpful to have the attachment questions used with the snack written out as well. It is useful to bring to session a list of the attachment-based play activities that the therapist has decided to use for that session. A sample session plan may look like this:

PLAY
- Double Double (clapping game) (touch and rhythm)
- Fast Slow clapping (mirroring)

- Breathe Together (touch, mirroring, rhythm)
- Row Row Row Your Boat (eye contact, touch, rhythm)
- Gentle Touch (touch)

TALK
- Continue Attachment Narrative

FEEDING AND QUESTIONS
- A time Mom had fun with her child
- A time the child had fun with Mom
- Something Mom did for her child this week
- Something the child did for their mom or family this week
- Something each looks forward to doing together in the future

A reminder that repetition of activities and questions is good and desirable across sessions throughout the therapy.

Working with Teens

M-MAT as described in this book is specifically designed for working with children 5 to 12 years of age. M-MAT elements, however, have been successfully implemented in working with teens and their parents, when an attachment injury was indicated.

Teens are, and should be, more autonomous than younger children. They are in a different developmental stage with a stronger need for differentiation from their parents. If they do not have a solid attachment base, however, they will struggle with this developmental task. They may be inappropriately clingy, or very hostile, or very disengaged from their parents. Underlying all this, there exists an injured child.

In working with teens, begin sessions with more limited attachment-based play, choosing older games such as clapping games and hand stack or mirrors. The therapist may choose to do only one or two games each session. Begin the talk portion with the Story of Love and move to the Attachment Narrative. The Attachment Narrative is well suited to teens. At this age they are able to contribute quite a bit to their story with the parent filling in the gaps, and parent and therapist supporting cognitive corrections and highlighting a helpful and adaptive story of the teen's life.

For teens, the attachment narrative usually takes longer than for younger children, both because they have had a longer life and because the teen is able to contribute much more to the conversation. The therapist can take time with the narrative. Teens are usually very interested in the telling of their story. The attachment narrative can be a very powerful tool in working with teens and their parents and it is not unusual for previously undisclosed trauma to surface when working with teens and parents on the attachment narrative.

As with younger children, the therapy can then move on to other talk topics such as skill building and behavior.

The session is ended with a snack and attachment questions. Some questions can target things the teen and parent are specifically working on, with a focus on successes. Appreciations and fun, however, are included as well (see Chapter 6: M-MAT Feeding and Questions). Thus, the frame is maintained and the parent and youth end on a positive note.

10

M-MAT Individual

Rationale

There are, unfortunately, many children who do not have an adult committed to them for the long term. Therapists may work with these children in shelters for abused and neglected children, foster family agencies, treatment programs and other similar settings. Therapists may also find themselves working with a child who is living with a permanent caregiver who is either unwilling or unable to attach to the child or commit to the therapy. Children with attachment injuries, who have no committed adult, are at great risk for life difficulties.

Multi-Modal Attachment Therapy Individual (M-MAT Individual) is designed for working with children with significant attachment injuries who have no appropriate, committed, long term caregiver; and who will be able to participate with the therapist at least weekly for at least 4 or 5 months. The target age of 5 to 12 years of age is the same as for M-MAT. As always, the therapist should start with a full assessment of the child to determine the child's needs.

The goal of M-MAT Individual, as in M-MAT, is still to help attachment injured children develop a template for positive relationships and the inner resources necessary to be successful in life. How is that achieved without a caregiver to work with? In the case of M-MAT Individual, the therapist engages in the attachment-based play with the child, to provide the needed touch, eye contact, mirroring and rhythm, to facilitate healing. It is important to note that the therapist is in no way trying to take on the parenting role. The therapist must always be aware of, and maintain, therapeutic boundaries. How to maintain boundaries while doing this work is described further in this chapter.

Some people may question the wisdom engaging in attachment-based play with the child, when the therapist is likely short term in the child's life. This is a legitimate concern and below are strategies to minimize emotional distress for the child. The M-MAT attachment-based play elements of safe touch, eye contact, mirroring and rhythm are desperately needed by the child and, when provided with appropriate boundaries, are healing in and of themselves.

There is the possibility that the child will develop an attachment to the therapist, and this is OK, and even a sign of health. Consider that the child with no template at all for relationship is at far more risk than the child with at least one experience, one positive template. Once the child has internalized one positive relationship with an adult, the child will have a better chance of being successful in future relationships and, therefore, in life in general.

M-MAT Individual Overview

M-MAT Individual is similar to M-MAT in many ways and is based on the same principles and concepts. To understand M-MAT Individual, first understand M-MAT as described in this book.

Similar to M-MAT, M-MAT Individual is a structured therapy employing both play and talk portions with the goals of healing relationship, developing a positive narrative and building skills.

Differences which will be discussed below include boundaries, structure, transferring attachment, and closure.

Therapeutic Boundaries

While many of the principles for M-MAT Individual and M-MAT are the same, working with an attachment injured child individually is very different from working with a parent in the room. When the M-MAT therapist is working with parent and child, the therapist is striving to support attachment and closeness between the parent and child. The parent/child relationship, however, is quite different from the therapist/child relationship. The therapist is a relative stranger to the child, and will likely not be forever in the child's life. The boundaries between parent and child, and therapist and child, therefore, are different. While the M-MAT therapist may encourage a child to climb into their parent's lap, the therapist would set appropriate boundaries if a latency age child tried to climb into the therapist's lap.

The therapist can help set boundaries and expectations by identifying him or herself as a "helper person" in the child's life. This can be done at the first meeting. The therapist can say something like, "I have a cool job. My only job is to help you! I don't get kids in trouble, I only try to help them. I can be a helper person in your life." If the child is in a temporary setting where the therapist is working, the therapist can further say, "While you are here, I will be one of your helper people." This sets a time frame and can later be used to distinguish between helper people and forever people in the child's life.

If the child has difficulty with boundaries, teach specifically to this, both in the moment and during the talk portion of the session. For instance, if a child the therapist just met indiscriminately jumps into their lap, the therapist can gently move them to the seat next to them and say something like, "Oh, let me shake your hand! I don't know you very well, and you don't know me very well, so we should shake hands. You only want to sit in the lap of people you know very well!" The therapist can then plan to teach to appropriate boundaries in the skill building part of talk therapy at a later time.

For each component of M-MAT Individual, the differences with M-MAT and how to maintain boundaries are discussed.

Session Structure

The M-MAT Individual sessions are structured similarly to the M-MAT parent/child sessions. There is a beginning, a middle and an end, with attachment-based play at the beginning, and questions at the end, framing the middle portion. The purpose of the structure is the same as for M-MAT, in that it creates consistency and safety and is therapeutic in and of itself.

One of the differences in individual therapy is the inclusion of a non-directive play portion, which occurs after the talk portion. It is useful to say, "First we will play my games, then we will play what you want to play!" If the therapist is working in a play therapy room with toys, the child will likely be drawn to the toys. This provides motivation for the child, and also allows the child further processing through play, while still allowing the attachment work. The session structure, with approximate times for a 50 minute session, is as follows:

1. Attachment-Based Play: The Frame Part 1 (5 minutes)
2. Attachment Talk: can include re-storying, skill building, psychoeducation and/or addressing behavior. (20 minutes)
3. Non-Directive Play (20 minutes)
4. Success Questions/Closing: The Frame Part 2 (5 minutes)

Of course the timing of each of the sections depends on what works for any given child. In general, a younger child will involve more play and less talk.

How each of these M-MAT Individual components is the same as or different from those in M-MAT is described below. Please read the earlier portions of the book to understand the components fully.

M-MAT Individual Attachment-Based Play

The implementation of attachment-based play between therapist and child is probably the component that most differentiates M-MAT Individual from other individual child therapies. The attachment-based play is the first part of the session and, along with the success questions, frames the middle talk and non-directive play sections.

The therapist engages in attachment-based play with the child and maintains boundaries, first by choosing less intimate, less threatening attachment-based play games. Appropriate games include clapping games, high fives, thumb wrestling, follow the leader games, and eye contact games (i.e., staring contests). One way to gauge this is to think about what games would be appropriate peer to peer. These games would likely be appropriate for the therapist and child. The therapist avoids games such as gentle touch and holding/rocking activities. Also, as in M-MAT principles, the child always has permission to not participate. In Appendix A: Attachment-Based Play Activities, games that are appropriate for individual therapy are identified with the letter "I".

There is no need to encourage touch outside of the attachment play. The therapist does not initiate hugs. If the child is overly physical, the therapist can use it as an opportunity to teach boundaries. If necessary, the therapist can teach a side hug, wherein the parties hug with one arm from the side, around the shoulders, for a count of three. The therapist can also substitute high fives or handshakes for hugs. Some children will avoid touch altogether outside of the attachment-based play, which is fine, and appropriate.

Though less intimate, the touch, mirroring, eye contact and rhythm in M-MAT Individual attachment-based play is still healing for the child.

M-MAT Individual Talk

M-MAT Individual Talk is the second part of the session and occurs directly following the attachment-based play.

As in M-MAT, the talk portion of M-MAT Individual includes re-storying, skill building, psychoeducation and addressing behavior.

Re-Storying

In M-MAT Individual, re-storying does not include the story of love, as that requires a parent. The attachment narrative also requires a caregiver in the room, so there is no pressure on the child and the child can just listen to the conversation, if that is their wont. The child may not be able to tolerate well a direct conversation with the therapist about their history, and, without a permanent, committed caregiver, the child does not have a secure base to support them.

The therapist can, however, address the child's history. The therapist should review the child's history outside the session to understand the themes of the child's story. The therapist can then plan out sessions to address those themes using story/metaphor, and psychoeducation. For example, if the child was exposed to domestic violence, the therapist can tell the story of April the rabbit, who lived in a rabbit hole where there was fighting all the time! In the story, the therapist wants to address empathy for the child (or character in the story), fault and responsibility, and possibly apology.

In a subsequent session, the therapist may provide direct psychoeducation about how children sometimes feel when the grownups around them fight, and why it is never the child's fault. The psychoeducation is provided without expecting anything from the child, allowing the child to play or draw if they wish while the therapist talks.

The therapist can also read to the child any of the many children's books that address themes with which the child may be struggling.

Because the therapist is a stranger to the child, addressing the child's history may come a little later in the course of individual therapy, after the therapist has developed some rapport with the child, and the child is demonstrating some comfort in the session with the therapist.

If a child brings up a challenging or traumatic experience from their past, the therapist can help the child process the experience, explore feelings, provide empathy and address the themes of fault and responsibility. Additionally, if appropriate to the situation, the therapist can offer an apology to the child as they might have had the parent do. This may look like this:

> I am so sorry that happened to you. If I had (name of perpetrator) here, I would have them get down on their knees and apologize to you. No adult should treat a child that way. As an adult, representing adults, I want to apologize to you that you were hurt like that. I am so sorry. You didn't deserve that. You deserve to be well cared for.

Skill Building

Skill building is the same in M-MAT Individual as in M-MAT, and includes self-regulation/self-soothing; feelings Identification and expression; communication skills; boundaries; and social skills as needed.

Psychoeducation

Psychoeducation regarding shame and guilt and clarifying responsibility is equally as relevant in M-MAT Individual as it is in M-MAT. Psychoeducation regarding parent/child roles may come up in relation to the child's current living situation, or their history, and should be discussed as needed.

Addressing Behavior

Behavior outside the session is addressed as needed. Whatever the child's living situation, they may be displaying behavior that is causing them a great deal of difficulty, and maybe even threatening their placement. Use acceptance and empathy to team with the child in assessing what is occurring and how to be more successful. Externalizing anger and the behavior, and CBT (Cognitive Behavioral Therapy) role play, as discussed in Chapter 7: M-MAT Talk, can be useful in achieving these goals.

M-MAT Individual Non-Directive Play

The third part of the session is non-directive play. M-MAT Individual differs from M-MAT in including non-directive play in the session.

While M-MAT Individual uses a non-directive play portion, it is not the same as Non-Directive Play Therapy. Non-Directive Play Therapy has its own set of protocols and principles which are often quite different from M-MAT Individual. Therapists can avail themselves of the many resources available regarding Non-Directive Play Therapy if they wish to learn more about this modality.

While non-directive play therapy, in and of itself, is insufficient for treating children with attachment injuries, when integrated into M-MAT Individual, non-directive or child centered play appears to be helpful. The non-directive play occurs after the talk portion and before the closing questions. It seems to give the child the space to integrate the information from the talk portion, and process in a different manner. It also provides some relief from the more intense interactional part of the therapy.

As in traditional non-directive play, the therapist can provide reflective comments. For M-MAT Individual it is not necessary for the child to engage in imaginative play activities. It is fine if the child wants to play a board game with the therapist, or read, or build with blocks. The child and therapist enjoying this time together in a way that is not pressured or goal oriented supports an appropriate attachment.

M-MAT Individual Success Questions

In M-MAT individual, the therapist includes the frame for the session, with attachment play at the beginning and success questions at the end, but eliminates the feeding portion, as feeding the child is more aligned with parental boundaries.

The questions, also, are not focused on relationship in the same way as they are with the parent in M-MAT. They are success oriented questions rather than attachment oriented. So, for instance, in M-MAT, the therapist may ask a child about a time they had fun with their parent. In M-MAT Individual, the therapist may simply ask about a time they had fun, or a positive experience they had that day; or the therapist and child may engage in a closing ritual of saying three good things that happened that week, or three good things about themselves. The therapist can also focus questions on successes the child is experiencing on therapy goals. Thus, the closing questions for M-MAT Individual are positive, but less relational. Hence, the closing questions in M-MAT Individual are referred to as success questions, rather than attachment questions as in M-MAT.

Though less relational, the success questions still serve the purpose of creating a new, success oriented, storyline or narrative for the child.

Transferring Attachment

If the child is moving to a permanent placement, then M-MAT with the child and new caregiver would be an ideal continuation of the therapy. In many circumstances, however, the therapist will not be continuing with the child in their new placement. If the child and caregiver can be referred to another therapist for M-MAT that would be the next best option.

If the therapist will no longer be working with the child, the therapist will want to provide several sessions with the child and caregiver during the transition, if possible. The therapist should endeavor to talk with the caregiver first to understand their commitment to the child and explain the purpose of the transition sessions to support the connection of the child and caregiver and the transition to the new home.

In the caregiver/child sessions the M-MAT structure is maintained with the frame and talk portions. The talk portion, however, focuses on the transition and the new relationship. The therapist can encourage discussion of the positive reasons the caregiver is taking the child into their home. The therapist can help the child express any concerns, questions and worries they might have. The therapist can explore with the child and new caregiver their hopes and wishes for the future and each other.

In the attachment-based play portion, the therapist can support the connection between the child and new caregiver through the play. If the new caregiver is not well known to the child, then the play should be appropriate to the level of unfamiliarity, similar to the guidelines for child/therapist play, and the therapist should participate as well. Appropriate boundaries should be maintained, and the child should not feel forced to participate. The goal should be to have some fun to support the new relationship, and, as always, the child's boundaries should be respected.

Closure

Not all children will develop a strong attachment to the therapist during M-MAT Individual, but some may. Given that the child has attachment injuries and may have developed some attachment to their therapist, it is particularly important how closure is handled by the therapist. Consistent with M-MAT principles, the therapist wants to pay particular attention to shaping the meaning the child makes of the closure. The child needs to walk away feeling that they are valued. This can be done in several ways.

One way is to use the last session with the child to honor the child and the relationship. This may include bringing a special snack or treat, and setting up a special activity. Creating cards for each other is a nice closing activity, with the therapist supplying a variety of materials, including glitter, stickers and markers. The cards then are given to each other during the session. It provides an opportunity for the therapist to write special things about the child in the card, and the card can become a transition object that the child can take with them.

It is also very good to provide an additional transition object for the child. While gift giving throughout the course of the therapy is counterproductive, during the last session, a special little gift, such as a special stone or other object, can serve as an additional transition object. One strategy for reducing the potential for distress at the possible loss of the object is to tell the child that the object represents the child's specialness, and good wishes for them, and even if someday they lose or misplace the object, it will not matter because the specialness and good wishes will still be there.

The child should also be acknowledged for any progress and successes they have made. In some instances the closure could be likened to a successful graduation.

The therapist should be talking to the child at least a few weeks before closure about the ending of the therapy. One way for the therapist to validate the child and make positive meaning is for the therapist to share both their feelings at the ending, and also their excitement for the child's future. The therapist needs to be genuine, and age appropriate for the child. This may look something like this:

> I am really going to miss you! I have enjoyed our time together and getting to know you. I am very excited and happy for you, though, because I know you are going to a home where you will get the care that you need and deserve!

For older children, if the therapist feels that the child has developed a healthy, positive attachment, they can use this as a reference point for the child saying something like:

> I feel like we have developed a good relationship. I feel like we respect and care about each other. This is good because now you know what this feels like to be in a good relationship. Although all relationships are different, you'll be able to know if a relationship feels like a good relationship.

The child may ask questions like, "Why can't I live with you?" or, "Can you adopt me?" This may be signs of a genuine attachment or of indiscriminate attachment. Regardless, the answer can be the same. After validating the child's feelings, the answer needs to focus on the therapist's limitations, and that the child deserves more. A possible response:

> You would like to come home with me. I appreciate that! I sure have enjoyed our time together. I'm afraid that I am only a helper person in your life, though. I'm not able to be there for you all the time. You deserve a forever home and someone who can be there for you all the time (if this is the plan for the child). You need and deserve more than I can give you.

It is also important to acknowledge and validate underlying feelings, and how hard goodbyes can be.

Appendix A: Attachment-Based Play Activities

Almost any playful activity that includes touch, eye contact, mirroring and/or rhythm will work for M-MAT play. Most games played with very young children will work. Avoid competitive and intellectual games. Be creative, but make sure the activity includes at least one of the critical elements: Touch, Eye Contact, Mirroring, Rhythm.

The relevant elements of each activity in this appendix are indicated by a letter following the description as so:

T: Touch; E: Eye Contact; M: Mirroring; R: Rhythm

Games that are suitable for M-MAT Individual (Multi-Modal Attachment Therapy - Individual) are indicated with an (I)

The following activities have been collected from multiple sources. A number of these games have been obtained or derived from Theraplay® trainings or materials. For more information on Theraplay® go to www.theraplay.org.

For the purposes of M-MAT, all attachment-based play must include Touch, Eye Contact, Mirroring and/or Rhythm. Any activities found online or through other sources should be evaluated for these elements before integrating into an M-MAT session. Other programs or sources, including Theraplay®, may have different criteria for attachment-based play, and some activities may not meet the requirement for M-MAT play.

Each game selected for a session should be repeated several times within the session before moving on to the next game. If the client and family have gained mastery in the game, some games, such as clapping games, can be altered to increase complexity or to go faster or slower, to add variety and challenge as needed. The games below are listed in alphabetical order.

All around the garden
Adult traces a circle on child's hand singing:
"All around the garden like a little mouse"
Then walks their fingers up the child's arm singing
"One step, two step"
Then runs their fingers up the arm for a gentle tickle under the chin with:
"In your little house"
(T R)

Baby powder hand or foot prints
Lightly powder the child's hands or feet and make prints on black or dark paper. (T) (I)

Blindfold touch walk
Child is blindfolded. Therapist stands on one side with their hands on the child's wrist and arm, and parent is on the other with a hand on the child's wrist and arm. Parent and Therapist walk with the child around the room. Therapist and parent take turns having the child touch different objects and child guesses what they are touching. I always have the child eventually touch the parent's hair or

skin and guess. If appropriate (child is old enough/safe enough), parent and child can change places. This activity requires a level of trust and is usually better a little later in the therapy process. (T)

Body part sounds
This one can be good for the reluctant child. The therapist or parent might discover that when they touch the child's foot it makes a "ring-a-ling" sound, and when they touch their nose it "beeps", etc. (T)

Breath together
Therapist, parent and child hold hands. Therapist leads and as they raise their hands, they breath in, and as they lower their hands, they breath out. Therapist can coach "nice deep breaths". (T M) (I)

Clapping games
Patty Cake, Double Double, or any other child clapping game will work. In these games you have both non-threatening touch and mirroring occurring. This can be done three ways with parent, child and therapist clapping together; or just between parent and child. You can find any number of clapping games online. (T R M) (I)

Clap patterns
Therapist starts by clapping a pattern. The parent and child repeat the pattern simultaneously in a call/response pattern. After therapist takes a few turns, the parent leads the clapping, then the child. (T R) (I)

Comparing body parts
A very simple game in which the parent and child compare the size or other aspects of body parts. For instance, putting hands up against each other's and seeing how big/

small each is, or seeing how high child's head reaches on parents' body, etc. Can also compare color, shape, freckles, etc. Can also introduce past and future orientation by saying things like, "Can you remember when your child's hand was even smaller than this?" or "I bet he may grow up to be even taller than you someday." (T M)

Eye blink pattern

Have the child look at the adult in the eye while the adult blinks a pattern (i.e., blink pause blink blink). The child then blinks the pattern back to the adult. The child can then have a turn to initiate the pattern. Very young children may find this too difficult. (E M) (I)

Eye color guess

Therapist tells parent and child, "Close your eyes and don't look!"

Then, "Now, without looking, Mom, can you tell me what color (child's) eyes are?"

"(To child) can you tell me what color your mom's eyes are?"

"OK, now open your eyes and take a look and see if you are right!"

Parent and child now look at each other's eyes.

"Can you see any other colors?"

This is a one time activity, often done early in the course of therapy, that encourages non-threatening eye contact. (E)

Feeling faces

One person makes a face depicting an emotion, while looking at the other person. The other person copies that face and guesses the emotion. This can also be done in a group where the face is passed around the group. It is then the next person's turn. (M E) (I)

Follow the leader

This can be done moving around the room in different ways. Or it may be more appropriate to do this sitting down where you move your hands (i.e. clapping, patting your thighs, etc.) and possibly head in a rhythmic pattern. I usually make changes on counts of four, or multiples of four, making it easier to follow. The child can have a turn to be leader after the adults. (M) (I)

Gentle touch

A very simple game to be used with children of all ages. I have at times used it every session as a closing to the play part of the session. Parent touches the child appropriately, gently, and child touches the parent back in the same way. It is then the child's turn to touch the parent in some appropriate way and the parent touches back in the same way. Repeat a number of times. This is one that the therapist usually stays out of. (T M)

Hand squeeze message

All participants hold hands in a circle. The first person squeezes the hand of a person next to them in some kind of pattern such as "squeeze squeeze pause squeeze squeeze". That person passes the squeeze pattern on to the next person in the group and it goes around the circle back to the first person who says if it comes back the same as it went out. I often instruct participants to close their eyes, or at least not watch the squeezing as it goes around the circle. I also instruct them to keep the pattern simple, usually no more than 5 to 7 squeezes, depending on the age/ability of the group. Note that the group may be just the parent, child and therapist. (T) (I)

Hand squeeze pattern

Adult and child face each other holding hands. Adult starts and squeezes a pattern, i.e., left, left, right, right. Child squeezes back the same pattern. Then it is the child's turn. (T M) (I)

Hand stack

Each person puts a hand in the stack and then their other hand, in the same order, so all the hands are stacked up. Then the person with their hand on the top moves it to the bottom, the next person does the same, etc. Start out slow. At some point you can reverse the order and the hand on the bottom moves to the top of the stack. Usually this game picks up speed until there is fun chaos. (T) (I)

Itsy bitsy spider

Sing the classic song, but facilitate parent and child doing movements together, i.e., each uses a hand and they work together to do the movement for the 'spider' moving up the water spout. This is tricky. Better for a little older child. (T R)

Mirrors

Child and parent, or therapist, face each other. First the adult moves slowly and child follows, then the child leads. I instruct parent and child to look in each other's eyes the whole time, and to see if they can move together so that I cannot tell who is leading and who is following. For older clients, The parent and child can pick who is going to lead without the therapist knowing, and then see if the therapist can guess who the leader is. This can be done either standing, or sitting just using hands and head movements. (E M) (I)

Mother may I
Played the usual way, but directions include things like, "hug your child and take one step forward" or "move up to where your mother is and give her a high five". If child is sent back to start, I invariably give direction to parent, "go back to start, take your child's hand, and bring him X number of steps forward". Complexity of directions depend on age and ability of the child. I always have them reach me at the same time. Parent then gets a turn to direct. In this game, I never give the child a turn to direct, saying they are too young to be the "mother," thus maintaining the hierarchy. (T)

Motor boat, motor boat
Participants stand in a circle holding hands. They move slowly in a circle singing, "motor boat, motor boat go so slow," they then pick up speed singing, "motor boat, motor boat go so fast," and finally, go even faster with "motor boat, motor boat step on the gas" until therapist or parent calls "stop" and they freeze, then do the same thing in the opposite direction. (T R) (I)

Peanut butter – jelly
One person says, "peanut butter," the others reply with "jelly" mimicking the same intonation/speed etc. They do this a number of times changing tone, pitch, and speed. (M R) (I)

Peek-a-boo
Classic peek-a-boo. This is a good one to use when the child is shy and hiding their eyes. The adult can engage the child with a playful, "Where is _____. There he/she is!" as the adult discovers the child. They can then allow the child to hide again and repeat. If the child is strongly withdrawing the adult can give the child

additional blankets , etc., to hide behind, thus going with, rather than against, the resistance, and maybe at first only discovering a foot or elbow. (E) (I)

Ring around the rosie (almost)
Hold hands in a circle and move clockwise or counterclockwise while singing the traditional "Ring around the Rosie" song, BUT at the end instead of "we all fall down," whoever is 'it' calls out a movement, such as "we all clap our hands" or "we all stamp our feet" and the participants engage in that movement, then it is the next person's turn. (T R M) (I)

Rock-a-bye- baby (almost)
Parent holds or rocks child in whatever way is appropriate and comfortable while parent and therapist sing traditional "Rock-a-bye-baby" song, BUT, replace the word "baby" with the child's name, and at the end, instead of "down will come baby, cradle and all" sing, "and we will catch *child's name* cradle and all." The therapist can direct parent and child to look at each other's eyes throughout the song, and repeat as appropriate. (T R)

Row, row, row your boat (almost)
Child stands or sits between parent and therapist. Parent and therapist hold hands making the 'boat'. Child puts their hands on the adults' hands as they row the boat to the song. Have the child facing the parent and ask them if they can look into their parent's eyes the whole time, singing the song:

Row, row, row your boat gently down the stream,
Merrily, merrily, merrily, merrily *child's name* is such a dream!
Repeat as you want. (T R E)

Run to Mom (or Dad)

The therapist sits in a chair opposite parent. The child stands in front of the therapist, facing away from the therapist and towards the parent. The therapist holds on to the child, arms around the child's waist, fingers laced, and challenges the child to run to their parent, who is waiting with open arms. Child, of course, eventually breaks through the therapist's arms and makes it to the arms of their parent. This is best done when the child is reasonably comfortable with the therapist, and is better for younger children. (T)

Silly faces

One person makes a silly face at the other person, then the other person copies it. They take turns. This one can also be done in a group, passing the silly face around the group. (M E) (I)

Stand up – back to back

Two people sit down on the floor back to back with knees bent and feet on the floor. They interlock their arms, and try to stand up. This is better for older children and will not work if the size between the people is too different. (T)

Stand up – face to face

Two people sit down on the floor facing each other with feet touching toe to toe, and holding hands. They try to stand up together. This is better for older children and will not work if the size between the people is too different. (T)

Thumb wrestling

If you do not know how to play this, ask someone. Make sure it is all in fun and not too competitive. A good way to engage child in non-threatening touch. Good for older children. (T) (I)

Touching body parts
One person calls out a body part, such as "elbow" and then everyone touches elbows. This is good both for dyads and larger groups. (T)

Touch guess
One person closes their eyes and the other person touches them as lightly as they can on their bare skin and they see if the person can feel it. Then they trade. (T)

Tracing shapes or letters on the back
One person traces with their finger a shape or letter on the other person's back, and that person has to guess the shape. Then they switch. I usually start out with piece of paper with six shapes drawn on it (i.e. square, circle, triangle, cross, star, zig-zag) and have the participants pick from that. When they demonstrate proficiency with this, they then use numbers or capital letters. (T) (I)

Twinkle twinkle (almost)
To the tune of Twinkle Twinkle Little Star adults sing to child:

Twinkle twinkle little star
What a special boy/girl you are
With (say some things about the child) i.e. long long hair
And a bright sweet smile
Strong strong legs
And a smart smart brain
Twinkle, twinkle little star
What a special boy/girl you are.

The adults in the room can use whatever special qualities about the child that they like. They can touch the child as appropriate on each body part that they are talking about and can trade off coming up with positive attributes of the child. (T R)

About the Author

Catherine Young, LMFT, is a Licensed Marriage and Family Therapist who has been providing therapy to children and families for well over 20 years. She has worked in a variety of settings including public and private mental health agencies, children's day treatment programs, children's shelters, adoption and foster care agencies, and private practice. She has further worked as a clinical supervisor, providing support for other therapists in their work with children and families.

You can contact Catherine at:

catherine@m-mat.org

46084953R00117

Made in the USA
Lexington, KY
22 July 2019